The
WILL *to*
LEAD,
the SKILL
to
TEACH

Transforming Schools at Every Level

ANTHONY
MUHAMMAD

SHARROKY
HOLLIE

Solution Tree | Press

a division of

Solution Tree

555 North Morton Street
Bloomington, IN 47404
800.733.6786 (toll free) / 812.336.7700
FAX: 812.336.7790

email: info@solution-tree.com
solution-tree.com

Printed in the United States of America

15 14   7 8 9 10

Library of Congress Cataloging-in-Publication Data

Muhammad, Anthony.
  The will to lead, the skill to teach : transforming schools at every level / Anthony Muhammad, Sharroky Hollie.
     p. cm.
  Includes bibliographical references and index.
  ISBN 978-1-935542-54-4 (perfect bound) -- ISBN 978-1-935542-55-1 (library edition) 1. School improvement programs--United States. 2. Educational leadership--United States. 3. Effective teaching--United States. I. Hollie, Sharroky, 1967- II. Title.

  LB2822.82.M85 2011
  371.2'07--dc23
                       2011038612

Solution Tree
Jeffrey C. Jones, CEO & President

Solution Tree Press
President: Douglas M. Rife
Publisher: Robert D. Clouse
Vice President of Production: Gretchen Knapp
Managing Production Editor: Caroline Wise
Senior Production Editor: Suzanne Kraszewski
Text Designer: Raven Bongiani
Cover Designer: Jenn Taylor

Acknowledgments

The acknowledgments for this book could easily be as long as the text. I have been so abundantly blessed, and there are so many people who have helped me grow in my short time here on this earth. First and foremost, I must give praise and all of the credit for anything worthwhile to Almighty God, the creator of all things. He has guided every step I have ever taken and every thought that I have ever produced, and to Him all praise is due. I eternally thank Him for H.E.M. and H.L.F., the two most influential figures in shaping me as a man.

I must acknowledge and thank the love and influence of my grandmother, Emma Roberson Harper (Madear), the matriarch of our family, the rock that we love and on whom we rely. Special thanks to Ann Nelson, my mother, nurturer, and friend. Donald Crawford, my father and twin, thanks for your spirit and DNA; we are much more alike than we would ever admit. Thanks to Andrew Nelson, Sr.; I appreciate you raising a son that you did not conceive when others would have run the other way. I extend a very special thanks to my beautiful wife, Dronda. I appreciate you showing me the other side of life and for all of your patience, love, and support. Carmen, thanks for giving me the four greatest gifts that a man could ever receive. Rashad, Larry, Jamilah, Shaheed, Ayanna, and Logan, the sun rises and sets on you. There is nothing that I would not do for you. Do not be afraid to take on the world and become what God created you to be. Angie, Lee, Donald, Brandon, and Derek (R.I.P), thanks for supporting your big brother. Cookie, Wendy, Billie, Peter, Birdie, Ricky, and Lori, thanks for supporting your nephew. Thanks to the entire Harper, Crawford, and Nelson families for your support and love. Special thanks to the Muhammads all over the planet. Thanks to the Gilliam/Hale family for accepting me into your family and giving me love and support.

Finally, I would like to give a special acknowledgement to my hometown of Flint, Michigan, the greatest place in the world for a young man to grow up. Wherever life takes me, I will be a Flintstone for life!

From a professional standpoint, I would like to thank the follow-ing people who have been powerful influences on me. Again, thank you, Mom, for being a great teacher and a great educational role model. I would like to express special appreciation to Dr. Richard DuFour for being a role model, a mentor, a friend, and one of the best educators this nation has ever produced. Becky DuFour and Robert Eaker, thank you for your guidance and willingness to share your wisdom with me. I would like to express appreciation to Jeff Jones, Donald "Stubby" McLean, and the entire Solution Tree staff. Dr. Freya Rivers, the first master teacher I ever observed, thank you for pushing and encouraging me, even when we did not agree. I would like to give a special acknowledgement to the Southfield, Michigan, Public Schools for your support and confidence, espe-cially the very special staff, students, and parents at Levey Middle School, the greatest middle school on the planet. I would also like to acknowledge all of the educators at Michigan State University for your wisdom and guidance. Finally, I would like to thank Dr. Sharroky Hollie for being a bold advocate for underserved children and for being a friend and a great colleague.

—Anthony Muhammad

I usually do not write acknowledgements for fear of forgetting someone. I am grateful to my family and support network for their patience and understanding about my passion for being an advo-cate for all underserved students, which keeps me from home regu-larly and consumed in one way or another while at home. I want to thank all of the educators who are responsive in their teaching and who show high will and high skill. Thank you for what you do and will continue to do on behalf of underserved students. You are making a difference! Lastly, I want to acknowledge Dr. Anthony Muhammad for his brilliance, courage, vision, generosity, humility, and invaluable contributions to schools and educators around the world.

—Sharroky Hollie

Solution Tree Press would like to thank the following reviewers:

Jill Colby
Principal
Sobesky Academy
Lakewood, Colorado

Amy Davies
Social Studies Instructional
  Teacher Leader
Taylor Allderdice High School
Pittsburgh, Pennsylvania

Roberto Gutierrez
Principal
Citrus Middle School
Orange Cove, California

Patrick Henry
Language Arts Department
  Chair
Thunderbird High School
Phoenix, Arizona

Patricia Lapinsky
Reading and Writing Coach
Starke Elementary School
Deland, Florida

Cindy Pilch
Assistant Principal
Afflerbach Elementary School
Cheyenne, Wyoming

Kristen Schroeder
Principal
James Sales Elementary School
Tacoma, Washington

Douglas A. Tyson
Principal
Joyce Kilmer Middle School
Springfield, Virginia

Table of Contents

PART III: THE SKILL to TEACH

About the Authors

 **ANTHONY MUHAMMAD, PHD,** is a much sought-after educational consultant. A practitioner for nearly twenty years, he has served as a middle school teacher, assistant principal, and principal, and as a high school principal. His tenure as a practitioner has earned him several awards as both a teacher and a principal. Anthony's most notable accomplishment came as principal of Levey Middle School in Southfield, Michigan, a National School of Excellence, where student proficiency on state assessments more than doubled in five years. Anthony and the staff at Levey used the Professional Learning Communities at Work™ model of school improvement, and they have been recognized in several videos and articles as a model high-performing professional learning community (PLC).

As a researcher, Anthony has published articles in several publications in both the United States and Canada. He is author of *Transforming School Culture: How to Overcome Staff Division* and a contributor to *The Collaborative Administrator*.

To learn more about Anthony, visit www.newfrontier21.com.

 **SHARROKY HOLLIE, PHD,** is a tenured assistant professor at California State University, Dominguez Hills, in the Teacher Education department. Sharroky teaches reading for secondary teachers, classroom management, and methodology. From 2007 to 2009, he was a visiting professor in diversity at Webster University in St. Louis in the School of Education. In Spring 2011, Sharroky was a guest lecturer at Stanford University.

Sharroky is the cofounder of the nationally acclaimed laboratory school Culture and Language Academy of Success (CLAS) in Los Angeles. CLAS is a K–8 independent charter school that espouses culturally-responsive pedagogy as its primary approach. At CLAS, Sharroky directs and develops the curriculum, professional development, and teacher development. Sharroky is also the executive director of the Center for Culturally Responsive Teaching and Learning, a nonprofit organization dedicated to providing stellar professional development for educators desiring to become culturally responsive, where he serves as a national expert, traveling around the country training thousands of teachers.

Sharroky is a featured author for Pearson publishing, coauthoring with Jim Cummins in the Cornerstone and Keystone series and contributing to its Prentice Hall anthology. His work has appeared in several edited texts, including *Teaching African American Learners to Read* and *Talkin Black Talk*. He is also the author of *Culturally and Linguistically Responsive Teaching and Learning: Classroom Practices for Student Success.*

To learn more about Sharroky, follow him on Twitter @validateaffirm, or visit his website, www.culturallyresponsive.org.

To book Anthony or Sharroky for professional development, contact pd@solution-tree.com.

PART I

WILL *and* SKILL

Introduction

he question of how to improve schools has long plagued practitioners, researchers, policymakers, and community members. Some have argued that the problem with low-performing schools is cultural—related to the people within the system and their beliefs, norms, attitudes, and behaviors (Green, 2005). Others have argued that the problem is structural—related to the structure of our educational system and its policies, practices, and procedures. They believe that low achievement is the product of a bad system (Viadero, 2010). We assert that it is a combination of the two—not one or the other—that has led to poor outcomes for students, particularly for struggling and underserved students, many of whom are from minority groups.

With the passage of No Child Left Behind in 2001, closing achievement gaps among diverse student groups became a focus of the federal government in the United States, as schools and districts were required to disaggregate student test scores and other performance data by student characteristics. This legislation created both a greater awareness of racial disparities and a rising concern about other kinds of achievement gaps, such as socioeconomic. In the decade since the law passed, most achievement gaps have not been closed to an appreciable degree, despite the introduction of more targeted interventions for different groups of students.

The National Assessment of Educational Progress (NAEP), an annual test distributed to a diverse cross-section of students in the United States, shows that, over time, Black and Hispanic students have made small strides in improving their performance in reading and mathematics, although their still exists a gap between their achievement and that of their White peers. For example, Black and Hispanic students trailed their White peers by an average of more than twenty test-score points on the NAEP math and reading assessments at fourth and eighth grade, a difference of about two grade levels (Annie E. Casey Foundation, 2011).

The problem of disparity among racially and economically diverse students does not stop with standardized testing. A National Center for Education Statistics report cited that while 82.7 percent of Asian students and 78.4 percent of White students in the class of 2008 graduated on time, only 57.6 percent of Hispanic students, 57 percent of Black students, and 53.9 percent of American Indian students graduated on time (Annie E. Casey Foundation, 2011). In addition, low-income and minority students tend to have less access to the most effective, experienced teachers with knowledge in their content field. One study of forty-six industrialized countries found the United States ranked forty-second in providing equitable distribution of teachers to different groups of students. For example, while 68 percent of upper-income eighth graders in the United States in this sample had math teachers deemed to be of high quality, that was true for only 33 percent of low-income eighth graders (Braeden, 2008).

We assert that, despite these statistics, student ethnicity and social class are not barriers to learning; rather, schools that do not properly respond to the needs of these students are the barriers. Schools must adopt a new, more comprehensive approach to ensure learning for all students, especially underserved minority students and those from poor communities: a healthy learning environment coupled with responsive learning activities developed around the specific needs of diverse students. This, we believe, is the right formula for universal school success. The student is the center of the school universe, and the learning environment and learning activities must be responsive to student needs if we are to avoid achievement gaps.

Will and Skill

It is our belief that successful school improvement requires that educators have a combination of both *will* and *skill* to ensure a quality education for every child in every classroom. *Will* is the belief that all children can learn and perform academically. Educators must be leaders of this will within their school culture. *Skill* is the use of responsive instruction that is the practical key to ensuring that students learn at high levels. For underserved students especially, it means engaging and reaching students on their own terms with attention to their cultural, home, and community experiences. Educators can have the will to lead, but if they lack the skill to teach, then student learning will fall short of our desired outcomes. Above all, our teaching must be tailored to student needs, not to the needs of educators.

The reform process that we advocate involves a combination of *will development* (developing the learning environment) and *skill development* (developing instruction).

Will Development

In chapters 2 through 5 of this book, Anthony explores the following elements of developing will.

Aligning the Philosophy

Schools are microcosms of our larger society. Educators' socialization plays a major role in their view of how the school should operate and whether or not they believe all students or a particular group of students will succeed academically. Successful schools recognize that educators come to school with different philosophical positions, and they seek to create a united professional paradigm for their organization in which there is alignment among staff members' beliefs, particularly about student success.

Managing Frustration

Frustration can undermine educators' best intentions. When a committed group of professionals creates lofty organizational goals, there will be obstacles that make accomplishing those goals challenging. Schools that recognize these obstacles and create norms and policies that effectively confront and minimize them increase their chances of developing a powerful and positive learning environment.

Creating a Culture of Collaboration

Philosophical alignment is meaningless unless it is accompanied by behaviors that reflect commonly held beliefs. This means creating an environment in which educators are compelled to align their behaviors with the needs of the student body. This step is very important in the development of a positive learning environment, and it must be done in collaboration.

Institutionalizing Cultural Health

Once a staff cultivates a culture with behaviors that meet the needs of students, it must create policies, practices, and procedures that reflect those beliefs and behaviors. This involves leadership at both the formal and informal levels, including teachers, site administrators, central administrators, and local and national policymakers.

Skill Development

In chapters 6 through 11 of this book, Sharroky examines skill development through the implementation of responsive pedagogy. His insight comes from his work as a cofounder of a charter school in Los Angeles—the Culture and Language Academy of Success (CLAS)—which has become a national model for culturally responsive teaching and is known for its success with underserved students, particularly African American students. Much of the content of this section of the book is based on the instructional practices implemented at CLAS. According to the California Standards Test and the Academic Performance Index (API), CLAS has maintained high achievement data, specifically in English/language arts, compared to the local district and the state. According to the API, CLAS scored an 822 for its elementary school and a 728 for its middle school in 2010. Additionally, nearly 60 percent of the students are advanced or proficient in reading/English/language arts according to the federal report card (adequate yearly progress, or AYP).

This section examines the following elements.

What Is a Responsive Pedagogy, and Why Is It Important?

Teachers often have many tools in their tool belts when it comes to working with students. However, they do not always use these tools responsively. Responsive pedagogy validates and affirms students and their cultural and linguistic background, creating a bridge to academic success. This responsive pedagogy differs from traditional one-size-fits-all strategies by seeking to engage students on a deeper level, thus drawing them into the learning process. It avoids deficit thinking and is suitable for not just struggling students, but all students.

The Steps to a Responsive Pedagogy

Three steps form the basis of developing a responsive pedagogy: (1) identify an area of instruction for improvement, (2) assess the quantity and quality of the activities currently used, and (3) implement responsive activities during teaching. These steps help teachers find their path from traditional only instruction to responsive instruction.

Four Instructional Areas for Responsive Instruction

There are four areas in which responsive instruction is most critical: (1) classroom management, (2) academic vocabulary, (3) academic literacy, and (4) learning environment. This book takes an in-depth look at responsive activities within these four areas that have been implemented with success at CLAS and in the authors' work with teachers and students, along with key philosophies, premises, and strategies on which responsive instruction in these areas is based.

⤳

We believe that will and skill must go hand in hand if schools are to improve. Educators must have the *will to lead* and the *skill to teach*. We challenge the traditional assumption that culture and structure are separate issues. We contend that educators must be engaged in creating a school environment with high will *and* high skill if students are to be successful. In addition, this cannot be done in isolation. All educators must be involved in the development of culture and pedagogy.

In their work on professional learning communities (PLCs), Richard DuFour, Rebecca DuFour, and Robert Eaker (2008) note that educators must (1) determine what they want students to learn, (2) decide how they will know if students have learned, and (3) determine how to respond when students haven't learned. The students who have not learned—the students who struggle and are most often underserved in our schools—are the targets of this book. To be sure, all schools face the issue of students who are not achieving—regardless of demographic profile. All students who struggle need a proper organizational response. However, in this book, we focus on the students who have been traditionally underserved by the current system.

The Blame Game

The traditional approach in education has been to blame the student, blame the parents, and blame society as a whole when students struggle. We challenge educators to look at themselves as not just a part of the problem, but as part of the solution. We ask readers to reflect on the following issues:

- Do some of my personal assumptions, beliefs, behaviors, and habits contribute to the underperformance of some of my students?

- Do my instructional practices or instructional leadership practices contribute to the underperformance of some of my students?

We do not advocate the ineffective strategy of blaming the client—students, parents, and society—rather, we encourage the grueling work of looking into a personal and professional mirror and asking what we can do to positively affect the lives of struggling young people.

Many great theories have emerged before this work, and we respect and recognize the contributions of others, but we also recognize that the standard approach to helping struggling students has failed, and we seek to reframe the conversation around new approaches to culture and pedagogy. School improvement begins with self-examination and honest dialogue around topics that are not often talked about, like institutional culture, personal beliefs and motivations, bias, discrimination, and cultural insensitivity. In this book, we do not duck those topics—we deal with them head on.

The "Turnaround" Concept

According to Tyack and Cuban (1995), the philosophy of public schooling in the United States is formed around two important and inseparable principles:

1. All children have the right to have their gifts and talents cultivated through the process of education.

2. All children can learn and become educated.

However, statistics reveal that all students are not realizing the promise of an educational system set up to meet their diverse needs. In a report released by the Thomas B. Fordham Institute and Basis Policy Research, of 2,025 chronically low-performing elementary and middle schools identified in ten states in 2003–2004, only about 1 percent had improved enough to exceed their state's average academic performance five years later, and fewer than 10 percent had even broken out of the lowest 25 percent of schools in their state (Sparks, 2010).

If we were to measure the current performance of the public school system against its stated objective, most would agree that the system has not met its goal. Additionally, we can agree that most struggling students within the system come from very predictable social groups identified by race, socioeconomic status, disability, and gender (Shaw, 2008). This lower-than-desired performance by schools and students has spurred an international debate about what it takes to turn a failing school around.

We believe failing schools can be turned around, and we believe developing the will to lead and the skill to teach—a focus on culture and structure—within every school is the key to this transformation. We infuse the concept of cultural responsiveness throughout this text because we believe that understanding the whole student is critical to properly serving the student. Teachers can use this understanding as a bridge when helping students achieve mastery of the academic curriculum. Effective schools meet the needs of the student. We argue that to truly close achievement gaps, schools must do this for all students, not just for some.

One

The Two Parts of a Positive School Environment

As we established in the introduction, successful school improvement requires that educators have a combination of both *will* and *skill* to ensure that students receive a quality education and have the best opportunities for success in school and life. Educators can have the will to lead, but if they lack the skill to effectively engage students, then student learning will suffer. Conversely, individual educators might possess the skills to teach effectively but lack the will to lead students and colleagues, causing inconsistent quality in education and adverse outcomes for student learning. A balance of the two, in what we call a high-will/high-skill school, creates a positive school environment, tailored to the needs of students rather than educators, that makes success for all students a reality—especially for students who have traditionally been underserved and struggle to learn.

Will

What is *will?* It is the power of making a reasoned choice or having control of one's own actions. It is characterized by determination, a certain attitude, or a particular desire or choice. Do all schools have the will to improve? Do all educators have the will to lead? Do all administrators and teachers have the desire to align their goals and intentions to the stated intentions of the organization? Unfortunately, the answer is no. All educators do not share a positive attitude about organizational reform. Desire, commitment, focus, positive attitude, and leadership are qualities that have to be cultivated, not left to chance, because they have a tremendous impact on student outcomes. Researchers Goddard, Hoy, & Hoy (2000) created a twenty-one–item efficacy scale to measure the level of individual teachers' belief in student achievement and a staff's collective belief in its ability to effectively teach students. They discovered that increases in teachers' belief in student achievement and a staff's belief in itself positively correlated with improvement in student learning. As Goddard and Hoy point out in their study, will is best when it is developed collectively as opposed to individually. Students are a part of a school *system*—not a one-room schoolhouse.

Collective will is also referred to as school culture. Kent Peterson defines *school culture* as the norms, values, rituals, beliefs, symbols, and stories that make up the persona of a school (Cromwell, 2002). School cultures fit into one of two types: healthy and toxic. A *healthy school culture* is a place in which:

> Educators have an unwavering belief in the ability of all of their students to achieve success, and they pass that belief on to others in overt or covert ways and they create policies, practices, and procedures that support their belief in the ability of every student. (Cromwell, 2002, p. 3)

Conversely, a *toxic school culture* is one in which educators believe that student success is based on students' level of concern, attentiveness, prior knowledge, and willingness to comply with the demands of the school, and they articulate that belief in overt and covert ways. In a toxic school culture, educators create policies and procedures and adopt practices that support their belief in the impossibility of universal achievement (Cromwell, 2002).

There is a direct link between the belief system of a staff and its behaviors and actions. A staff that aligns its intentions around student achievement develops a commitment to the essential behaviors that have been proven to boost student performance. A healthy school culture does the following:

- Fosters a commitment to staff and student learning

- Emphasizes accomplishment and collaboration

- Celebrates successes

These qualities are essential in highly impactful schools. They are the catalyst for meaningful problem solving, professional development, pedagogical experimentation, and collective goal setting (Cromwell, 2002).

Skill

Creating highly effective schools requires more than will—it requires specific action to bring vision into reality. This leads us to the next question: what is skill? *Skill* is a great ability or proficiency, an art or a craft. Education is an art *and* a science that requires the development of organizational skill—the ability of a staff to tailor its professional skills to the specific needs of the students it serves. Robert Marzano (2010) identifies the instructional skills of teachers as "the cornerstone of school effectiveness" (p. 2). He identifies effective teaching in every classroom as a critical commitment to creating meaningful school reform (Marzano, 2009b). Researcher Carol Cummings (1996) describes the challenge of effective teaching as using a web of specific skills: "Teaching is so complex! It involves classroom management, long-term planning, use of materials, human relations, and knowledge of content as well as instructional skills" (p. 12). Cultivating these diverse skill sets requires consistent and focused professional development. They are not developed by happenstance. Part III of this book addresses developing this skill set—responsive instructional practice structured around the norms, values, and culture of the student—and highlights specific strategies and activities that fit within this paradigm.

This combination of a healthy organizational will and a well-defined and refined set of professional skills will help us address the inequity of student achievement that has adversely affected millions of students. With this comprehensive strategy, we can best help those students who struggle to learn.

The Four Zones of a Positive Learning Environment

A positive learning environment is marked by the proper blend of will and skill and leads to the development of supportive structures and instruction for students. Schools can fall into one of four categories in their balance of will and skill: high will/low skill, high skill/low will, low will/low skill, and high will/high skill.

High Will/Low Skill

A school with high will and low skill is a school in which the staff's beliefs and attitudes have been aligned with the stated objective of the school—learning for all—but the skills to manifest this belief have not been developed. This staff has an optimistic attitude about student potential without the ability to cultivate that potential. An overemphasis on student feelings and relationships has overshadowed the importance of developing instructional skill and academic rigor. A typical high-will/low-skill school has the following characteristics:

- Many student celebrations and acknowledgements for nonacademic achievements

- An optimistic attitude toward students and their emotional needs, but no focus on rigorous academic tasks or higher-order thinking activities during instruction

- A staff that values relationships with students but has few expectations for student performance that stretch beyond a student's comfort zone

- Low emphasis on collecting or examining student learning data and frequent attacks on the validity of outside measures of student performance

A school that places its efforts solely on the emotional needs of learners and neglects their academic skills may make students feel good temporarily, but will leave them unprepared for the competitive environment they'll enter after graduation. This school has failed to make student learning the cornerstone of its purpose, and in the long run, students suffer.

High Skill/Low Will

A high-skill/low-will school emphasizes acquisition of knowledge only and discounts the power of motivation and relationships. In a high-skill/low-will school, a student is simply a receptacle for information. Educators in these schools believe their responsibility stops when they fill the student with information. If the student cares to learn, he or she has the opportunity to learn; if a student chooses not to learn, the student must be willing to accept the consequences for his or her choice. High-skill/low-will schools have the following characteristics:

- A very refined and complex curriculum

- Staff members with a high level of knowledge who take pride in their knowledge and experience

- Staff members with many personal achievements, but few students with achievements

- High numbers of students failing academically and little to no support system for struggling students

- Staff who do not support students' emotional and personal development

- Combative relationships between staff members, students, parents, and administrators

- An administration that protects and supports the status quo environment

These types of schools may be fertile ground for technical educational jargon and high academic standards, but high standards alone do not produce great results. The staff of a high-skill/low-will school does not see the need to cultivate its students. Customer service is not important to these educators. They view the personal qualities students need to adequately process instruction and meet high academic expectations—such as perseverance, focus, and commitment—as qualities students should develop outside of school. A staff member in a high-skill/low-will school thinks about the educational process in the following way: "It is my job to teach and the student's job to learn." This perspective misses one simple but critical principle, however: children may not have the intellect or maturity to cultivate personal qualities on their own—they often require the guidance of a caring and qualified adult.

Low Will/Low Skill

A school characterized as low will/low skill is quite honestly the worst-case scenario for students and staff. The school does not function well on any level. There is very little belief in students either socially or academically, and educators in these schools also lack the skill to cultivate students academically. In fact, the combination of low skill and low will leads to a sense of contempt among educators and students and parents. A school categorized as low will/low skill has the following characteristics:

- Low academic standards
- Low student achievement
- High numbers of student conduct violations
- High numbers of students who are failing academically
- High turnover among teaching and administrative staff
- Adversarial relationships between staff members and students and parents

Low-will/low-skill schools are our most dysfunctional and underperforming schools and the focus of great concern since the passing of No Child Left Behind. They violate the stated purpose of public education. Policymakers have been confused on how to deal with these schools that some call "dropout factories" (Thornburgh, 2006). Some advocate for punitive measures, while others advocate support. What is obvious is that no one benefits—neither students, educators, parents, nor society as a whole—from low-will/low-skill schools.

High Will/High Skill

A high-will/high-skill school is an organization that has matched its belief systems with its practices. There is a philosophical agreement that all of its students have the capacity to become successful, and the educators spend their time and energy seeking and implementing practices that are best suited to manifest their collective goal of learning for all. A high-will/high-skill school has the following characteristics:

- Staff members with high academic expectations for all students

- Staff members who value relationships with students and use students' backgrounds and experiences as a bridge to high academic success

- Staff members who respect the culture of their students and collaborate to become responsive to students' specific needs

- A philosophy in which student support is an integral part and institutionalized in the school's policies, practices, and procedures

- Staff members with high level of skill in classroom management, academic vocabulary, academic literacy, and learning environment who pride themselves on their knowledge and experience in these areas

- Staff members who reflect on the quality and effectiveness of their instructional strategies

- Staff members who believe that learning for all is the only acceptable outcome

The Need for Philosophical Agreement

Many researchers identify this need for philosophical agreement as critical to student success. In their PLC model, DuFour et al. (2008) identify shared mission, vision, values, and goals as a critical characteristic of learning communities—the will components. This forms the foundation for their additional characteristics: collective inquiry, collaborative culture, action orientation and experimentation, continuous improvement, and a focus on results—the skill components.

A comprehensive study of effective characteristics of high-performing schools in high-poverty areas (Petrides & Nodine, 2005) found that effective schools possess a clear understanding among all staff, teachers, and administrators of the district's performance goals concerning student achievement, and the alignment of organizational processes and systems to meet those goals. Douglas Reeves's (2000) analysis of highly successful schools in Milwaukee known as 90/90/90 schools (90 percent minority, 90 percent students living in poverty, and 90 percent academic proficiency on state assessments in both math and reading) found that these schools shared common characteristics, such as a focus on academic achievement, clear curriculum choices, and frequent assessment of student progress and multiple opportunities for improvement. The research shows a common thread: effective schools align educational philosophy among staff, and they move swiftly to align professional practice with that shared philosophy. This book seeks to establish a clear and effective path to accomplishing both.

Reeves also establishes that student and school performance is *multivariate.* He states, "Those who claim that a change in one variable causes a change in another variable have usually not scratched the surface of the issue at hand" (Reeves, 2000, p. 8). In other words, there is no one magic solution to the complex problems of schools. School reform is both cultural and structural. Schools and districts that understand the complexity of both facets and develop them appropriately are effective in reaching their goals. Those that rely on one in the absence of the other endanger the learning of their students.

Embracing Culture and Structure

In this chapter, we have established what it means to be a school with high will and high skill and shared the characteristics of these schools to show how these environments can impact student achievement. In the next chapter, we will delve more deeply into the specifics of school will and healthy culture. Before you move on to the next chapter, take time to reflect on the questions that follow.

CHAPTER 1
Reflections

1 Rate your personal will and commitment to educate every child. Do you have personal or professional barriers to believing that every child is capable of success?

2 Rate your professional skill as an educator. Are there areas of skill that you need to address? Rate your colleagues' professional skill. Are there areas of skill your colleagues need to address?

3 In which zone of performance is your school and/or district: high will/low skill, low will/high skill, low will/low skill, or high will/high skill? What evidence did you use to make this assessment?

4 What is your school's and/or district's greatest area of need—will or skill?

PART II
The WILL *to* LEAD

Conflicting Wills

During the ongoing debate about educational equity, few have stopped to ask, "Does everyone truly want every child to succeed?" As educational professionals, we would hope that every one of our peers truly desires to see all students succeed, but is that a wise assumption? Is it possible that organizational goals for student success may conflict with some employees' personal goals? Synthesizing and aligning all of the various ideologies of individual educators into one functional organizational philosophy is not an easy task.

Schools as Microcosms

Some scholars have argued that schools are simply a reflection of society. If a community embraces equity, justice, and freedom, then these qualities will be reflected within the walls of the schools. In that situation, schools can be an environment in which egalitarianism flourishes. If those qualities are absent on the outside, however, or they are unevenly distributed, schools will reflect that reality as well.

In *The Bell Curve* (1994), Richard Herrnstein and Charles Murray argued that the goal of creating a system that provides an equal education to all students is not only impossible, but detrimental to the betterment of society. They argued that all people are not evenly endowed and pouring resources into less-capable students unfairly and adversely affects the growth of more capable and gifted children.

In the past, many scholars identified schools as the perfect places to guarantee social and economic division. They argued that schools' primary purpose was to maintain comfortable social norms (particularly for the rich) and train others to prepare for and accept their place at the bottom of the economic ladder (Bowles & Gintis, 1976).

Yet others see schools as agents of social change. Researcher R. W. Connell (1993) places schools right in the center of social development. He argues that schools should *impact* society—not be *impacted by* society. He notes that within a progressive society, the public education system is a major asset. As one of the largest industries in a developed economy, it is paramount to the future development of society. He also notes that teaching is a "moral trade," and teaching and learning are social practices involving questions about authority and application of knowledge.

Scholars and practitioners do not always agree on the philosophical points, yet the research on high-performing schools identifies philosophical alignment among practitioners as the first step toward better practice (DuFour et al., 2008; Petrides & Nodine, 2005; Reeves, 2000). So the school change process has to start with the development of a productive and collective will, while recognizing that practitioners will come to school with many different personal ideologies shaped by their own experiences.

The Importance of a Healthy School Culture

In the book *Shaping School Culture: The Heart of Leadership,* Deal and Peterson (1999) write:

> While policymakers and reformers are pressing for new structures and more rational assessments, it is important to remember that these changes cannot be successful without cultural support. School cultures, in short, are key to school achievement and student learning. (p. xii)

There has been debate about the meaning of school culture. Some have mistaken culture to be synonymous with ethos, morale, and spirit. School culture is much more concrete than that, however. It is the deep patterns of values, beliefs, practices, and traditions that have been compiled and normalized over the course of the school's history (Stolp, 1994). School culture sets the standard for what is normal and expected in a school. It is multifaceted with patterns of values, beliefs, practices, and traditions. Staffs in school cultures rooted in high expectations for student performance will spend most of their time nurturing that expectation, just as staffs in schools with cultures of low student expectations will validate that norm.

School culture affects student learning and performance in many different ways. The National Center for Leadership looked at the effects of five dimensions of school culture: (1) academic challenges, (2) comparative achievement, (3) recognition for achievement, (4) school community, and (5) perception of school goals. In a survey of 16,310 fourth-, sixth-, eighth-, and tenth-grade students from 820 public schools in Illinois, researchers found support for the proposition that students are more motivated to learn in schools with strong cultures (Fyans & Maehr, 1990).

Researchers analyzed the effects of school culture on student achievement when they examined one school project directed at improving elementary students' test scores. The school project they studied focused on creating a new mission statement, goals based on outcomes for students, curriculum alignment corresponding with those goals, staff development, and building-level decision making. The results were significant. The number of students who failed an annual statewide test dropped by as much as 10 percent (Thacker & McInerney, 1992).

As this research shows, a school's collective norms, expectations, and values are tightly linked to the productivity of its students. Therefore, the development of a healthy culture cannot be left to chance. Educators must nurture and cultivate it methodically. It is important to note that schools with an organizational belief system that matches the norms and beliefs of a vast majority of their students can take this issue for granted. For example, when a school population consists of students who come from family environments that nurture values like high academic achievement, delayed gratification, and compliance with rules, students' socialization process matches the school's expectations. But other students come from families that do not share and cultivate what the school values—perhaps there is a lack of supervision and motivation for high achievement and adherence to rules. It can become politically expedient to ostracize and justify failure among this seemingly insignificant minority of students because they just don't "fit in" (Ogbu, 2003). This phenomenon can easily turn a stated mission of "learning for all" into "learning for most."

A metaphor helps to clarify the importance of culture as it relates to will and skill: culture is the soil, and organizational structures and practices are the seeds. There are certain conditions that soil must meet if the planter expects to harvest produce. If the soil is unhealthy, it doesn't matter how good the seed is. In fact, a healthy seed can be planted in dry, acidic, and uncultivated soil, and it will be just as unproductive as an unhealthy seed. *Seeds are only as good as the soil in which they are planted; likewise, school structures and practices are only as good as the culture in which they are implemented.* Structural change that is not supported by cultural change will always be overwhelmed by the unhealthy culture (Muhammad, 2009). Healthy culture provides the right environment, but does not guarantee effectiveness; it must also be accompanied by high levels of professional skill.

Toxic School Culture

The antithesis of a healthy school culture is a toxic school culture. Kent Peterson (Cromwell, 2002) describes a toxic culture in these words:

> Toxic school cultures believe that student success is based solely upon a student's level of concern, attentiveness, prior knowledge, and the willingness to comply with the demands of school and they pass that belief on to others in overt and covert ways. Toxic cultures also create policies, practices,

and procedures that support their belief in the impossibility
of universal achievement. (p. 5)

Toxic school cultures have a dominant belief system that places success or failure solely on the shoulders of outside forces. In his definition, Kent Peterson identifies four student characteristics that are prerequisites for school success: concern, attentiveness, prior knowledge, and compliance. Any educator would agree that these are important assets in the learning process and that not all students arrive at school predisposed to these characteristics. In toxic cultures, students are blamed for not possessing these characteristics, which releases adults from the responsibility of properly educating every student. This mentality is in direct conflict with the objective of public schools—learning for all. Toxic cultures essentially establish that some students are educable and some are not. Obstacles to student success are not viewed as challenges that adults must overcome; rather, they are products of home and community and therefore not the concern of the staff. Toxic cultures are said to be *descriptive* because educators within them become very adept at identifying every obstacle they face. Toxic cultures are *deflective* as well because they assign blame elsewhere—the staff itself is never responsible. Typically these schools spend their time blaming students, parents, the government, and others for problems instead of spending time trying to solve them (Butler & Dickson, 1987).

It is important to note that a culture is not considered healthy or toxic based on the type of problems the school faces. In fact, all organizations have problems (Collins, 2001) that are as unique as the people within the organization. What makes a culture healthy or toxic is members' collective ability to work together to solve problems. No organization can be successful blaming its clients instead of serving its clients.

Collective Commitment to Success for All Students

Healthy school cultures develop a collective commitment to student success. How do they accomplish this? They are courageous enough to recognize the profundity of their personal differences, but they accept that these differences are not as important as meeting the educational needs of their students. They are willing to confront the subtle but powerful assumptions that guide their worldview, the harmful stereotypes that interfere with a staff's ability to effectively focus on the development of each student—the elephants in the room.

There are three important "elephants" or barriers staffs must confront in order to develop the type of collective focus necessary to properly educate every child. These barriers are sometimes referred to as *predeterminations*. There are three types of predeterminations: perceptual, intrinsic, and institutional (Muhammad, 2009). If unhealthy predeterminations are present in a school, creating a system of equitable achievement is nearly impossible.

Perceptual Predeterminations

The first elephants to confront are the disadvantageous predeterminations about students—the perceptual predeterminations. These are often the long-held stereotypes of teachers. Stereotyping is a natural function of the human mind. Stereotypes help us to understand a complex world in simple terms. As Langlois et al. (2000) note:

> To help simplify a complex world, people develop mental models called schemas. Problems arise when people begin to oversimplify schemas. Oversimplified schemas are known as stereotypes. Stereotypes are fixed impressions and exaggerated and preconceived ideas and descriptions about a certain type of person, group or society. (p. 390)

People create mental models to understand how the world works on a daily basis, and they can become fixed about certain groups of people. Stereotyping does not make a person inhumane or unethical—it is a natural function of the human psyche. It is problematic, however, when mental models adversely affect our actions, specifically when they negatively affect the students educators are entrusted to serve. These stereotypes can include negative beliefs based on variables such as student race, sex, home language, disability, social class, and immigration status. Educators do not lose their right to their own opinions when they choose their profession, but it is ineffective and unethical for them to operate from a mindset that adversely affects the students they serve.

In a comprehensive study of five middle schools involved in restructuring in Philadelphia, Wilson and Corbett (2001), authors of *Listening to Urban Kids: School Reform and the Teachers They Want,* document that teacher expectations and perceptions about student performance greatly affected their practice. The students identified that teachers who "stayed on them and made them be successful" provided a rich learning environment (p. 64). Wilson and Corbett also found that these teachers that students identified as invested in their success "involved students in constructivist and experiential learning, and experienced better student conduct, grades, and scores on standardized tests" (p. 42).

Wilson and Corbett also describe teachers with negative images and stereotypes of their students. One teacher noted that she was scared of her students because she had never been in an urban environment and described her experience as a "daily battle between teacher and student for classroom control" (p. 34). Teachers with these negative stereotypes about their students tended to have higher job turnover, and, despite the district's investment in brain-based and research-based instructional strategies, these teachers "opted to rely on instructional strategies that were primarily suited to one style of intelligence rather than to several" (p. 34). One student described his experience like this:

> My science teacher is scared of us so we mostly work out of the book. We do vocabulary. We read the chapter and get the vocabulary words. After each section in the book, we do a section review. (p. 43)

The student is experiencing a low-quality education because of his teacher's assumptions about race, culture, and social class. The teacher's fear of and negative perceptions about African American students and their culture not only creates an unproductive learning environment, but also directly affects the level of pedagogy and content rigor in the classroom.

Educators' perceptions of their students have a profound effect not only on their will to teach students, but also on the methods they use to do so. The students in these five middle schools had totally different educational experiences based upon their teachers' perceptions. The schools that students rated more favorably had teachers who treated them with respect, listened to them, affirmed their identity, and pushed them to succeed. The clear difference between the ineffective and effective schools in this study was the effectiveness of school leadership in nurturing an optimal learning environment.

Intrinsic Predeterminations

Educators are only a part of the school community. Students' perception of self—intrinsic predeterminations—help to shape collective focus and will. If educators form broad and rigid assumptions based on their personal experiences and societal messages and images, it would seem natural that students would develop similar stereotypes about themselves. An African American boy who is consistently confronted with images of Black men as criminals in the media might come to believe that that is his destiny. A teenager who has grown up in a rural or isolated community where she is not exposed to a world that is growing and full of possibility may not be motivated to strive for excellence in school because she does not see how it applies to her life.

When seeking to develop a positive organizational will—a collective focus on success—educators must be up to the challenge of not only changing some long-held negative stereotypes about students, but also helping students overcome long-held negative stereotypes about themselves. A student's negative perceptions of his or her ability will affect his or her behavior and productivity. One study about the influence of student self-perceptions on achievement (Akey, 2006) concluded:

> The earlier schools and teachers begin to build students' confidence in their ability to do well, the better off students will be. Because students' perceptions of their capacity for success are key to their engagement in school and learning, schools should be designed to enhance students' feelings of

accomplishment. Teachers whom students see as supportive
and who set clear expectations about behavior help create
an atmosphere in which students feel in control and confident about their ability to succeed. (p. iii)

In addition, teachers have a difficult time educating students
who have these negative perceptions about their place in school
and their ability to excel. Michael Fullan (2003) identifies *student
engagement* as the first critical step in the educational process. It is
not surprising that a student with a negative self-perception about
his or her potential to succeed academically would have difficulty
engaging in the learning process.

Educators must transform their perceptions before they can help
students transform their intrinsic predeterminations. Research
on highly effective schools shows us that adults' will for student
success has to be stronger than the student's will to fail (Green,
2005). Students must believe in their ability to achieve their goals.
This concept, commonly referred to as *efficacy,* is a prerequisite
to effectively changing students' negative self-image. As Gardner
(1998) states, "Fostering self-efficacy, helping people to believe in
themselves, is one of an educator's highest duties" (p. 1).

Institutional Predeterminations

Finally, a school must be willing to analyze internal barriers to
achieving a collective commitment to learning for all. This means
confronting institutional predeterminations. No organization can
achieve a positive will with policies, practices, structures, or procedures in place that make achieving collective goals more difficult.
Educators at every level must sit down and reasonably review standard policies and procedures and align them with organizational
goals. For example, institutional policies such as student tracking
that limit access to rigorous coursework can be huge obstacles
to developing an optimal learning environment, especially if stereotypes and bias about certain subgroups of students keep them
locked into lower tracks where they do not have the opportunity
for success.

Healthy cultures recognize that there will be obstacles to creating high-will organizations, and that some of those obstacles are products of educators' perceptions, students' perceptions, and long-established organizational barriers. Instead of spending their time complaining about the issues, healthy cultures seek to understand the barriers and address them. In other words, a healthy culture is a community of problem solvers.

Abolishing Conflicting Wills

In this chapter, we have discussed the differences between a healthy school culture and a toxic school culture and discovered that school cultures are influenced by the predeterminations of the professionals and students within them, as well as the larger society of which they are a part. Institutional barriers also play a role in the health of a culture.

A staff's willingness to examine, debate, and synthesize the diverse paradigms in its school is the first step in developing a healthy and collective vision for the school. Educators must be willing to transparently communicate their commitment to students as it relates to their stated mission and challenge one another to live up to that commitment. This may require in-depth analysis of staff and student handbooks, discipline policies, instructional policies, and school norms. If these organizational policies do not support their efforts to educate all students, they must be willing to collaborate to revise them. Staff members must work to achieve a system that respects and nurtures the full potential of each student. There can be no split agendas. The sole focus must be on the well-being of the students they serve.

In the next chapter, we examine staff frustration and its significant impact on school culture. Before you move on to the next chapter, reflect on the questions that follow.

CHAPTER 2
Reflections

1   How have your personal experiences affected your perception of the field of education and the students you serve?

2   Based on the definitions of healthy and toxic school cultures, how would you rate your current reality? Do structural changes seem to flourish or flounder in your environment?

3   How have the three forms of predetermination—perceptual, intrinsic, and institutional—manifested themselves in your professional environment? What has your staff done to address these issues?

4   Do you and your colleagues tend to be more descriptive or prescriptive in your approach to solving problems?

Three

Frustration in a Toxic Culture

A highly frustrated staff is a highly ineffective staff. School staffs made up of members with high levels of frustration soon develop into toxic cultures, making the job of serving the needs of all students nearly impossible. School leaders and practitioners concerned with improving schools must understand the effect of frustration on school culture and professional practice.

What is frustration, and why is it so damaging? *Frustration* is the feeling of anxiety we get as a result of our inability to accomplish a task or fulfill a want or need. There is a gap between our desired outcome and the results we achieve. In schools, our desired outcome is universal student achievement. This is not a wish, but a requirement. In the United States, No Child Left Behind dictates that students must achieve better learning outcomes or schools risk losing self-governance and funding (Kopkowski, 2008). Educators are being asked to do things that they may not be prepared to do (Kennedy, 2005), such as ensuring student mastery of a complex curriculum, classroom management, formative assessment and data analysis, and academic interventions. A 2006 survey of American teachers found that 58 percent felt that these requirements were impossible to meet (Feller, 2006). Mandating outcomes in an environment in which educators may not have the skills to reach those outcomes can lead to several problems, including lowering academic standards and cheating on standardized tests (Dewan, 2010).

We must start to examine and fix the factors that lead to high levels of educator frustration. Pressuring people to do things that they do not know how to do will not improve productivity. This approach has only created a revolving door of educators in the schools that most need consistent, compassionate, and skilled educators (Sparks, 2002).

Insufficient Preparation

It is difficult for teacher preparation programs to simulate all of the conditions that a new teacher will face in the classroom (Moir, 2008). This lack of proper preparation can easily be linked to low job satisfaction and high teacher turnover (Associated Press, 2003).

A future teacher who is well versed in general theory will not necessarily have the specific skills needed for diverse classroom situations. Other fields, like medicine and law, recognize the importance of specialization of knowledge and the practice of specialized skills. A doctor not only has to complete a course of study, but he or she also must engage in daily practice—an internship and a residency— and pass special board examinations to be licensed to practice. An attorney must also spend years completing a similar battery of specialized practice and then must pass a comprehensive examination before being licensed. We are not suggesting that a person needs eight years of practical experience before becoming an educator; rather, we believe future educators must experience more specific development both inside and outside of teacher education programs to reduce potential frustration once they enter the classroom as professional teachers. Teachers who teach underserved students, for example, often enter the field without proper knowledge of how to best engage and reach these students. We will address this issue of responsive instruction in the second half of the book.

In one study of new teacher experiences (Kopkowski, 2008), five primary areas of dissatisfaction that cause high levels of frustration emerged:

1. Lack of support

2. Student discipline issues

3. Low pay

4. Lack of influence regarding school operations

5. Lack of respect from colleagues, administration, and parents

It is easy to understand why any person confronting all of these issues at one time would become frustrated. These unexpected barriers are overwhelming to new teachers as well as experienced educators.

One additional area that is not addressed significantly during teacher preparation is training in multiculturalism. Achievement data shows that students who have teachers from similar ethnic and socioeconomic backgrounds as themselves perform better than students who have teachers from different ethnic and socio-economic backgrounds (Viadero, 2008). A careful analysis of school achievement data from 1950 to 2000 shows that students who are White and middle class outpace other students who are non-White and impoverished in all tested academic areas (Gordon, Piana, & Keleher, 2000). A U.S. Department of Education (2005b) report titled *Eight Questions on Teacher Recruitment and Retention: What Does the Research Say?* reported that "it would be ideal if every teacher taught in an environment that matched his or her skills, back-ground, and temperament. This is a particularly serious problem for low-income and minority students" (p. 17).

At first glance, it may seem that the solution is simple: hire more educators from diverse ethnic and socioeconomic backgrounds. However, the problem is not that simple. The U.S. Department of Education estimates that 84.3 percent of America's teachers are White, while White students make up only 61.2 percent of the student population. Black students make up 17.2 percent of the student population, and Black teachers account for only 7.6 percent of the teacher workforce. Latino students make up 16.3 percent of the total student population, while Latino teachers account for only 5.6 percent of the teacher workforce (Toppo, 2003). Thus, trying to match the race and social class of teachers to the race and social class of students is mathematically impossible. So, we must do a better job preparing the current workforce of teachers to properly understand, motivate, and educate an increasingly diverse population of students. Understanding a student's norms, values, and beliefs is a great asset to an educator, and if the educator does not acquire this knowledge independently from his or her own life experiences, schools have to carve out time and resources to compensate for this gap (Howard, 2006). This means that a staff has to be willing to become "students of its students" and embrace professional scholarship. This can be accomplished through the principle of collective inquiry, or the collective search for best practices advocated through the professional learning community process (DuFour et al., 2008).

A school's ability to properly develop, socialize, and retain new teachers is critical to teachers' long-term performance and the organization's health (Barnes, Crowe, & Schaefer, n.d.). Typical obstacles that educators face, such as high standards from federal mandates and poor working conditions, are enough to make the first few years of practice in the field frustrating. Adding issues of culture and social class in an increasingly diverse environment requires that we look at preparation more seriously now than we have in the past.

Overwhelming Conditions

The current political climate in education has an increasingly adverse effect on educators' frustration and stress level. The achievement mandates in math and reading under No Child Left Behind, coupled with decreases in school spending, have caused many educators to express high levels of dissatisfaction (Bakst, 2008). Teachers and school leaders are being asked to accomplish more with fewer and fewer resources. The act of simply mandating reform, and then piling reform on top of reform, has proven to be detrimental to improvement (Christensen, Horn, & Johnson, 2008).

Lawmakers and some school leaders have failed to realize the effects these conditions have on school culture. From a theoretical standpoint, it is rational to believe that people should adjust to changing conditions, but we cannot forget that adjustment is not necessarily an easy endeavor, and many people resist change. If educational policy continues to be crafted without consideration of these conditions, frustration can only increase, guaranteeing a perpetual cycle of failure for students trapped in such a toxic culture.

Feeling overwhelmed is not a productive mindset for an individual, and it is even worse when that feeling is shared by large numbers of professionals within the same organization. Vandenberghe and Huberman (1999) refer to this phenomenon in schools as "work and responsibility overload," which they define as "not having sufficient time or capacity to complete all assignments and tasks" (p. 169). The many factors that lead to this overload accumulate over time. They include the following (Vandenberghe & Huberman, 1999, p. 167):

- Student violence
- Classroom discipline
- Apathy
- Overcrowded classrooms
- Unreasonable or unconcerned parents
- Public criticism
- Public demands for accountability
- Excessive paperwork
- Loss of autonomy and sense of professionalism
- Administrative insensitivity
- Bureaucratic incompetence
- Deficiencies in the physical environment

Vandenberghe and Huberman also point out that these stressors do not stop in the classroom. Administrators at both the site level and central administrative levels articulate similar stressors. Their level of dissatisfaction because of workplace and responsibility overload is just as profound. The researchers concluded that overworked and underprepared administrators have a hard time completing complex tasks.

It is important to note that Vandenberghe and Huberman conducted their study before No Child Left Behind was passed in 2001, so the list of stressors has undoubtedly increased since then. This increased frustration compelled one group of seventy-five educators from North Carolina to drive to Washington, DC, to speak with their congressmen about the issue. One teacher stated that the law "has taken the joy out of teaching" (Carpenter, 2011). The combination of inadequate preparation and overwhelming work conditions is a substantial catalyst for increasing frustration.

The Cycle of Blame

Frustration has an adverse effect on all members of the school community—students, teachers, administrators, and parents. In these environments, people do not effectively communicate and problem solve. Schools with high levels of frustration spiral into a cycle of blame—a state of total organizational denial in which members of the organization become satisfied with complaining about stressors and problems and blaming other members of the organization for those stressors and problems. A *cycle of blame* is a stalemate between members of an organization resulting from a collective inability to solve pertinent issues. Cultures locked in the cycle of blame are the most toxic and most difficult to change because no one recognizes his or her role in the toxicity of the school. Instead, members use their energy describing how others contribute to the toxic culture.

Schools locked in this cycle are like two kindergarten students involved in a squabble. Young children cannot reflect on their personal role in a dispute. Rather, they blame one another, each telling the teacher how the other student wronged him or her. These young children may be very angry and then pout about the problem, and then they get into a similar situation the next day.

While examining the nature of toxic cultures in chapter 2, we established that they are descriptive and deflective. The foundation of the cycle of blame is deflection. Everyone recognizes the stressors and issues, but deflecting blame onto others is easier and more comfortable than self-reflecting on the issue and taking on a challenge that may appear to be insurmountable. This deflecting of blame to others is a defense mechanism (Kramer, 2010). These mechanisms are psychological strategies used by healthy people "to cope with reality and to maintain self-image . . . to protect the mind/self/ego from anxiety, social sanctions or to provide a refuge from a situation with which one cannot currently cope" (Kramer, 2010, p. 271). According to Kramer, a defense mechanism is pathological "only when its persistent use leads to maladaptive behavior such that the physical and/or mental health of the individual is adversely affected" (p. 271).

When a person's need to feel adequate clashes with external forces too great to overcome, the result is a barrage of protective defense mechanisms and deflections. The combination of complex new tasks, fewer resources, and increased pressure and anxiety without consideration for human emotion can lead to disaster. For example, pressure to improve academic achievement at low-performing schools can be overwhelming for teachers when coupled with obstacles such as a lack of administrative support, students who are not concerned about achievement, and parents who are not involved.

Psychologist Serge Doublet (2000) identifies the issues confronting highly frustrated schools caught in the cycle of blame. He notes that people commonly mistake *being in control* with *being prepared*, and he states that deflection and blame are defense mechanisms developed out of a need to be in control. Doublet paints this picture very well with the following passage:

> The idea of "being in control" is not really a solution to stress or change; in fact, it is actually the cause of all the problems associated with the demands of stress or change in the first place. To understand this, let's begin by distinguishing "being in control" from thinking ahead, or "being prepared," because many persons confuse these terms. If you have to make a long trip through the desert, for example, packing survival equipment and a set of tools is good preparation. The preparation has nothing to do with being in control because no amount of preparation can prevent your car from breaking down. But being prepared for a breakdown

can reduce the difficulty of coping with it, and it can make the entire trip more relaxing. (p. 46)

As Doublet suggests, being able to respond to problems or issues is much more beneficial than seeking to control them and then lamenting the fact that we cannot control them.

A Culture of Complaint

When a person is highly frustrated, often his or her first inclination is to seek others who share similar frustrations. The old proverb is true: misery loves company. Schools are notorious for these kinds of interactions among staff members, especially as it pertains to students and parents. Some dismiss this as "venting," which implies that it's a harmless habit. In reality, persistent complaining has a significant impact on school operation and effectiveness, and certainly on school culture and will.

Complaining cannot be confused with protest. *Complaining* is an expression of pain or displeasure, finding fault in someone or something, or making an accusation. *Protests* are expressions of disapproval stated positively that speak strongly against something or someone. Complaining comes from a need to assign blame to others, while protest is rooted in a personal or professional disagreement. Disagreement and philosophical debate are important elements for organizational growth. We develop new ideas and clear conclusions when we debate issues from multiple perspectives (DuFour, 2001). Complaining, on the other hand, has no value. It comes from a need to deflect responsibility for anxiety onto others.

One study sought to understand the role of complaining in social interaction (Alicke et al., 1992). Researchers tracked the daily complaints of participants for a year and examined the root causes and goals of the complaints. More than 75 percent of all complaints were *noninstrumental*—they were not directed at changing an existing state of affairs. Rather, the complaining was done with the primary goal of venting frustration and reassurance (to solicit sympathy). Complaints most frequently targeted another person's specific behaviors, and those responding to complaints most often agreed with complainers' statements. The researchers concluded that complaining is a coping mechanism of people who are too afraid, and in some cases unqualified, to overcome the immediate obstacles in their paths.

Hopefully, we can all agree that complaining to our colleagues to deflect blame and reassure ourselves that we are not responsible for problems or their solutions is not the best way to behave when seeking to create a productive organization; however, this is exactly how people in toxic cultures operate.

Doing *to* Students Versus Acting *With* Students

What effects does a highly toxic culture with frustrated staff members have on students? Kent Peterson's (Cromwell, 2002) definition of a healthy culture states that collective norms and beliefs manifest themselves in policies, practices, and procedures. In other words, the philosophy of the educators will eventually become a part of the formal structures and practices of a school.

Members of a toxic staff feel a need to control their environment. Toxic cultures view their students as unproductive and uncooperative—as problems that need to fixed or controlled. As a result, toxic cultures develop and implement practices and policies that do something *to* students, rather than seeking cooperation *with* students. Healthy school cultures, on the other hand, view their students as clients, and they seek to develop practices and policies that best serve students' needs to ensure their success. We will explore this concept much more fully in the next chapter.

In toxic school cultures, students tend to be punished for a wide variety of behaviors, including poor attendance, lack of attentiveness, inappropriate conduct, not having paper and pencils, and even for not meeting financial obligations like paying book fines or cafeteria bills (Wren, 1999). Ronald Ferguson (1998) describes these schools as "quasi boot camps" that place more emphasis on student control than cognitive development. Rules, regulations, and student demands are posted clearly in these schools, but evidence of proficient student work and student-centered activities is rarely seen.

One policy that has been the topic of much debate is the practice of mandating school uniforms in public schools. David Brunsma (2004) analyzes this issue in his book *The School Uniform Movement and What It Tells Us About American Education: A Symbolic Crusade.* He asks the following key questions:

- Why are public schools, which have traditionally operated without rigid dress restrictions, suddenly implementing student uniform policies?

- Why have these policies been concentrated in areas with high minority populations, highly impoverished populations, or schools receiving low standardized achievement scores?

Brunsma found that districts with uniform policies say they mandate them for the following reasons:

- To reduce violence and behavioral problems
- To foster school unity and improve the learning environment
- To reduce social pressures and level status differentials
- To increase student self-esteem and motivation
- To help parents save money on clothing
- To improve attendance
- To improve academic achievement

This rationale appears logical; any school devoted to the pursuit of academic excellence for every student would agree with fostering those goals. However, Brunsma found that the actual results of such a policy never matched the stated objectives. He found that not only are school uniforms ineffective in meeting those ideals, but they can create negative outcomes; in actuality, school uniform policies exacerbate the issues they try to eliminate.

For example, most public schools with uniform policies serve urban populations. Typically, these are schools that serve poor and minority students and have often been identified as failing. Uniform policies make students in these schools easily identifiable from their more affluent, White counterparts who attend suburban schools where uniforms are less likely to be required. Schools require uniforms because principals, parents, and school boards want to control certain factors to have a more positive effect on the learning environment and student achievement; however, no empirical data support these outcomes. Research does not support uniforms as a method for improving individual student performance and behavior or schoolwide climate. So, the underlying purpose of uniform policies is to mark students' social ranking and class status as inferior, which makes these policies discriminatory and racist. Indeed, as Brunsma concludes, the issues that plague the public school system are complex and cannot be addressed through controlling what students wear to school.

Healthy school cultures are less concerned about doing *to* students and controlling fringe issues, such as student dress, and more concerned about working *with* students by being prepared to address the diverse challenges students face, such as improving their literacy and numeracy skills, so that all students can be successful.

Lessening the Frustration

As we've discussed in this chapter, frustration among educators who face ever-increasing responsibility and dwindling resources adversely affects school culture and student learning. Highly frustrated educators seek others who share similar frustrations, leading to a culture of complaint in which educators validate their anxiety and work to develop policies, practices, and procedures that control their environment, rather than working together to transform it. Education leaders must recognize that to ignore the psychological and sociological effects of frustration is to doom their policy objectives to failure from the start, and it is the students who suffer the most.

In the next chapter, we present a framework for transforming school culture from toxic to healthy. Before you continue to the next chapter, reflect on the following questions.

CHAPTER 3

Reflections

1   On a scale of 1 to 5, with 1 being low and 5 being high, how would you rank your personal level of frustration? How would you rank your organizational level of frustration?

2   When you and your colleagues are frustrated, do you tend to use one another as resources or as sounding boards to share frustration? How can you process your frustration in a more productive manner?

3   Do educators in your environment get the preparation, support, and training necessary to reach the goals expected of them? If not, how can you share these issues with your supervisors in a way that can help get you what you need to be successful?

4   Do you consider your organization a culture of problem solving or a culture of complaint? Why?

5   When under pressure, do you and your colleagues tend to do things *to* students or *for* students? If you tend to be more punitive than supportive, what supports can you provide for students that would help them grow?

The School Culture Framework: Creating a Culture of Collaboration

rameworks help us understand how abstract ideas inter-act with one another and make things that are difficult to describe more rational and more easily analyzed. In an attempt to better understand what makes schools toxic and healthy and how we can develop schools into positive learning environments, we use a framework described in depth in the book *Transforming School Culture: How to Overcome Staff Division* (Muhammad, 2009). The framework described in this chapter identifies the groups of educators within a school who jockey for the control of the collective norms and expectations within the school culture. They operate within two distinct spheres, greatly impacting the will of the school and its level of health or toxicity.

The goal of this chapter is to help educators understand how to create a culture of collaboration. A collaborative culture is one in which members of a school community "work *interdependently* to achieve *common goals*—goals linked to the purpose of learning for all—for which members are held *mutually accountable*" (DuFour et al., 2008, p. 15). We want to explore how a school can transition from a vision of learning for all into the practical application of that vision. This process starts first with recognition of what creates disunity and what needs to be done to foster unity.

The Players

In a typical school culture, staff members fit into one of four categories: Believers, Tweeners, Survivors, and Fundamentalists. These players in school culture have the power to influence one another in both positive and negative ways and have differing agendas that affect their behavior in unique ways. When not properly cultivated, these diverse agendas can lead to division and dysfunction—a toxic school culture in which no one possesses the will to lead students or their colleagues.

Believers are educators who are predisposed to the ideas and programs that support the egalitarian idealism of education. They use and seek out the best professional models to support the universal achievement of their students.

Tweeners are educators who are new to school culture. They are typically teachers who have just completed their education or certification or who are new to a particular school. They do not belong to one of the other three categories yet—they will usually "choose sides" within two to five years. This group is critical to school improvement because schools—especially high-risk schools—want to retain them. If schools do not retain qualified staff members, school reform is nearly impossible because long-term initiatives die out without organizational memory.

Survivors are educators with one purpose: survival. This group is made up of professionals who are simply "burned out" and so overwhelmed by the demands of the profession that they suffer from depression and merely survive from day to day. This group is much smaller than the other three, and there is a general consensus that this group needs more help than what is available in most schools and districts. They seek no alliances with other staff members and need the help of medical and psychological professionals to heal from the psychological effects of burnout.

Fundamentalists are educators who are comfortable with the status quo and organize and work against any viable form of change. Their goal is to be left alone. They have many tools that they use to thwart reform initiatives, and without the proper leadership, they are generally successful in that subversion. Fundamentalists see their personal needs and goals as more important than the needs of the students and the organization as a whole.

The interaction of these complex groups of individuals makes school reform difficult at best. School leaders must be disciplined and persistent to focus school professionals on the singular goal of success for all students. This is the critical piece in transforming the will of a school staff from low to high. We focus specifically on the interaction between the Believers and Fundamentalists because their influence most directly affects the health or toxicity of a school culture.

Believers and Fundamentalists

We've already established that researchers agree that high-performing schools have clear goals and high expectations for all students (DuFour et al., 2008; Petrides & Nodine, 2005; Reeves, 2000), which are found in healthy cultures. The critical question is, How do schools develop healthy cultures, and how do they continue to evolve without spiraling into toxic cultures? We argue that in order to accomplish this goal, schools must increase the number of Believers and increase their influence while reducing the number of Fundamentalists and neutralizing their effects on school culture.

An analysis of the behavior of Believers and Fundamentalists reveals a difference in philosophy and agendas that drive their behavior. Jim Collins, in his breakthrough book *Good to Great* (2001), identifies why great companies and organizations consistently outperform average or low-performing companies and organizations. He describes great organizations as having three strengths:

- Disciplined people
- Disciplined thought
- Disciplined action

When examining the issue of disciplined people, Collins writes:

> We expected that good-to-great leaders would begin by setting a new vision and strategy. We found instead that they first got the right people on the bus, the wrong people off

the bus, and right people in the right seats—and then they figured out where to drive it. The old adage "People are your most important asset" turns out to be wrong. People are not your most important asset. The right people are. (p. 12)

People and their commitment, focus, attitudes, and behaviors have to be aligned with the organizational objectives, or progress is nearly impossible. We do not subscribe to Collins's notion that there is a "right" person or "wrong" person. We believe that people are not innately or inherently right or wrong for a job. Their personal and professional experiences can shape their readiness to produce as much as their inherent ability, so leaders can cultivate and develop staff members' abilities and productivity to greater levels.

Those who display productive organizational behavior are the Believers, and those who display unproductive behavior are the Fundamentalists. It is this behavior that affects the will of the school, educators' ability to lead, whether a school culture is healthy or toxic, and, ultimately, whether the learning environment is a positive one in which students can succeed.

Believers know that their role is to help the organization achieve its objective—success for every student. Their focus on that objective guides their behavior, so constructive feedback does not spark a defensive response in them. They want to be prepared instead of in control. Simply stated, the organizational goal supersedes their individual goals. They are on the bus, in the right seats, and ready to lend their gifts and talents to confront obstacles and achieve collective success. A Believer is a true team player; a "we first" rather than a "me first" professional. If every educator behaved this way, research-based practices would be implemented with fidelity, and we would see the student achievement results that we crave.

Fundamentalists believe that their personal agenda is more important than the collective agenda. Protecting their personal and political issues becomes more important than the needs of the students they serve. They play political games and lobby other members of the organization to buttress their power base, and any reform efforts that are in conflict with their personal needs or desires become the object of their destruction. Fundamentalists lobby for issues like professional autonomy (especially in curriculum and assessment), professional ease, and work benefits like salary or extra benefits, for example. They lobby against complex tasks (even when they benefit students), changes to systems, and changes to protocol (like grading systems, parent contact protocol, and class size). A Fundamentalist is a "me first" and "we second" employee.

John Wooden, the late and legendary basketball coach at UCLA, was asked about what it takes to be a good team player. His response was to "consider the rights of others before your own feelings, and the feelings of others before your own rights" (Orr, 2009). Schools are teams of educators with the goal of educating every child. Selfishness and a focus on personal agendas are harmful to accomplishing that collective goal. Unfortunately, Fundamentalists have been allowed to hijack the focus, energy, and commitment in many schools within our school system. Fundamentalism and healthy cultures cannot coexist.

We advocate that leaders target these staff members in their efforts to build a collective will within the school because these team members are the source of the toxicity. Transforming the toxic behavior into better and more productive behavior is the focus of chapter 5.

The behavior of Believers, Fundamentalists, and all school professionals occurs within two distinct cultures: the collegial culture and the managerial culture.

Collegial and Managerial Cultures

Schools are complex organizations with many layers of human interaction. Education professionals wear many hats—sometimes they make decisions that affect others, and sometimes they are affected by the decisions and actions of others. This occurs within two distinct cultures of the school system: the collegial culture and the managerial culture. Breaking down the barriers between these two parts of school operation is paramount in the development of healthy school cultures.

Collegial Culture

The *collegial culture*, or informal culture, refers to the regular, informal interactions that professionals have with their peers. While engaged in this part of the organization, people tend to feel more comfortable with authentic communication because of perceived shared norms and the lack of a person who holds authority over the group. Membership is exclusive to those sharing similar rank and philosophy. Changing rank or philosophy may risk a person's membership in this group. The collegial culture is by far the most powerful part of the organization. This is the place where educators form covert alliances and lobby for their agendas. Everyone in a school or school system belongs to a collegial culture, and the health of this part of the organization is critical to creating a healthy culture.

It is not surprising that this group exists. Groups of people who come together regularly start to organize patterns of acceptable behavior—a series of norms and values. Over time these understandings become a framework—a guide for what it means to be a member of the group. The framework, once accepted by the group, becomes a requirement for membership and defines acceptable behavior within the group. It becomes the group's culture. People who are new to the group watch for clues on how to act (Goffman, 1959).

Lobbying takes place within the collegial culture, and it can be very dangerous to a healthy school culture, damaging the will of a staff. *Lobbyists* act on behalf of a group, trying to persuade others to support certain initiatives. Fundamentalists are the most active and effective lobbyists in a school culture, especially in the collegial culture. Conversely, Believers generally choose to isolate themselves instead of becoming actively involved in influencing the thinking and behavior of their colleagues. If a school hopes to have a healthy culture, Believers have to be more active lobbyists in the collegial culture.

Fundamentalists are very adept at rallying others to support agendas of personal interest to them, even though these agendas may not be in the best interest of students or the organization. This lobbying takes place informally in places like the teachers' lounge and parking lots and at informal gatherings. Formally, it takes place within unions and boards of education and as policy-makers leverage their influence to create adult-friendly legislation around issues such as funding and student accountability. This formal and informal lobbying has led some within the public to have negative perceptions about educators, that teachers are more concerned with their own agendas than with helping children achieve success.

Communication in the Collegial Culture

Collegial cultures have a communication system. Leaders who can access and influence this communication system are a great asset in transforming a school culture. The communication among members of a healthy collegial culture is very different from communication in a toxic culture. As we have previously noted, educators in a toxic culture develop a language of complaint. In these cultures, staff members share common criticisms of their work environment and consistently reinforce those criticisms in their communications. They consistently seek one another in informal situations to vent about their recent frustrations, which makes them feel validated, but does nothing to solve the problem. Healthy collegial cultures, on the other hand, develop a culture of problem solving. Members recognize that their commitment to organizational success demands that they utilize their informal communication system to build capacity rather than soothe egos (Muhammad, 2006).

A problem-solving culture expresses the understanding that problems will always exist—it's how we process and react to those problems that matters. When faced with the most daunting chal-lenges, such as low test scores, student discipline problems, and combative parents, the educators in a healthy collegial culture display an unusual calm that allows them to analyze the problem, hypothesize ways to handle it, and develop possible solutions to eliminate it. Healthy school cultures have a coolness that is very easily observed (Cromwell, 2002). Members of these cultures do get tired, angry, and even frustrated, but their resolve does not change. If you were to listen in on the conversations in a group of educators in a healthy collegial culture as they face a challenging situation, you might hear the following phrases:

- Why do you think we had an increase in student failure in math?

- What do we need to do to address this issue?

- Which teachers had a high level of success in this area? Are they willing to share their strategies?

- Who needs to get involved to solve this problem?

Just as healthy collegial cultures have a distinct style of communication, so do toxic cultures. A toxic culture's language is rooted in frustration and emotion and assigns blame for problems to external forces. Members do not own problems and collaborate to solve them. This way of communicating does not create an environment that nurtures self-reflection and collaborative organizational movement. When listening in on a conversation about a challenge in a toxic collegial culture, you might hear the following phrases:

- These students are the problem! Where is the support from home?

- Can you believe that nothing is being done about this? Someone needs to do something about this!

- I don't know why we even try! Nothing will change!

If phrases such as these are a regular part of the interaction between staff members, the culture is toxic, and no meaningful growth will happen until the paradigm of that culture changes. Toxic environments do not allow anything of value to grow. Change must happen at every level, but the most powerful place to start is in the collegial culture. Individual teachers who make an effort to change their communication style can make a difference within the collegial culture and thus impact the entire school culture.

Managerial Culture

In the *managerial culture*, members control the policies, practices, and procedures that affect others within the organization. For a teacher, this means control over his or her classroom. A site administrator has direct control over the policies, practices, and procedures in a school, while central or executive administrators have control over the formal affairs of the system. Each professional in a school culture belongs to a culture of peers and colleagues, but he or she also serves a formal managerial role that places him or her in a different role. Managerial culture is important in school reform because in order to develop a healthy culture, leaders at every level have to recognize the impact of their decisions on the beliefs, attitudes, assumptions, and behaviors of those they lead.

All behavior is motivated—it has an intended outcome that is personal and specific to the individual (Glasser, 1998). Leading others requires leaders to take some personal responsibility for the success or failure of the people they lead (Bolman & Deal, 1995). Leaders that simply give instructions and expect productivity are not qualified to transform a school culture.

In *The Six Secrets of Change: What the Best Leaders Do to Help Their Organizations Survive and Thrive* (2008), Michael Fullan's first secret, or leadership principle, is "love your employees." At first glance this notion may seem too emotional, but Fullan's explanation reveals that this strategy is a complex one:

> Loving your employees is not just about caring for employees. It is also about what works to get results. It is about sound strategies linked to impressive outcomes. One of the ways that you love your employees is by creating the conditions for them to succeed. (p. 25)

A good leader invests in the success of his or her staff. In a healthy culture, this happens at all levels—from administrators at the district level to individual teachers at the classroom level. Good leaders provide those they lead with formative feedback and allocate resources to help them improve, such as instructional coaching for struggling teachers or mentors for new administrators. If leaders adopt this outlook, frustration and stress will go down. People will feel more satisfied. This positively affects overall culture, moving the school from toxic to healthy—from a low-will to a high-will culture.

It's important to note that the behavior and language of the collegial culture is influenced by the behavior and language of formal leadership (Baldoni, 2007). Leaders set the tone in formal settings for how their staffs will communicate and handle problems in informal settings. Their behavior helps shape the language of the collegial culture. Leaders who take an external view of responsibility and communicate that view to staff will find themselves with a staff that is also reluctant to take responsibility. Starting formal communication with "The central office is making us . . . ," for example, is not a good way to encourage teachers to be self-reflective and solve problems. The leader who helps his or her staff reflect on the moral and professional purpose for a behavior or policy is much more likely to gain universal commitment for change. These leaders use language that reinforces a commitment to the betterment of "our students," which is likely to increase staff buy-in and help unite the staff members in their common purpose.

Reducing Fundamentalism

Most Fundamentalist behavior is an adverse response to a history of improper leadership. The school culture framework (Muhammad, 2009) we mentioned earlier in the chapter identifies four levels of Fundamentalism:

- Level-one Fundamentalists—These staff members resist change because they were never provided with a clear rationale for change. They do not understand the philosophical reasoning behind change initiatives, so they tune out change because it has no personal validity. Level-one Fundamentalists often exist because leaders have poor communication, and there is a lack of transparency.

- Level-two Fundamentalists—These staff members distrust their leaders. They become apprehensive about the validity of changes and reject them because of this distrust. They may feel like their leaders do not trust them.

- Level-three Fundamentalists—These staff members experience task overload. Their feelings of being overwhelmed and underprepared cause them to become fearful, anxious, and apprehensive about participating in the change. Leaders of level-three Fundamentalists often fail to properly develop their staff members' skills and resources.

- Level-four Fundamentalists—These school personnel have a need to be defined as oppositional. Their social status among their peers is based on resistance, and thus cooperation would redefine who they are—even if leaders have properly communicated rational, fostered trust, and provided adequate training. The only tool leaders can use to lead these staff members is coercion, creating a battle of wills.

Leaders can reduce the first three levels of Fundamentalism with effective leadership, usually without conflict and without destroying the professional relationship. As Porter (1961) noted, if the stimulation can be changed, so can the response. Reducing the fourth level of Fundamentalism requires leadership, but leadership of a different kind. Management pioneer Frederick Taylor (1947) wrote that "the principal object of management should be to secure maximum prosperity for the employer" (p. 174). Ultimately, a leader has to hold people accountable for their behavior and for achieving organizational results. As Fullan (2008) articulates, a leader is responsible for the development and cultivation of those that he or she leads, but that investment has to ultimately achieve tangible results.

Employees who thrive on being oppositional require strong monitoring and authoritarian leadership. For example, school leaders often have control over teaching assignments, and they can ensure that Fundamentalists are not rewarded with the most coveted positions. Once leaders have established an environment for productive behavior, they must require appropriate performance from these staff members, in spite of their personal feelings or commitments.

The behavior of Fundamentalists is detrimental to developing a healthy school culture—it can make a positive learning environment impossible. Even so, the focus of leaders must be on changing behavior, not targeting individuals. Leaders must focus on maximizing productivity within their schools and reinforcing the success of their employees by building up the Believers.

Building Up the Believers

The drama surrounding Fundamentalist agendas reduces precious time educators should be using for student-focused work, such as developing formative assessments, analyzing student learning data, and providing academic support for struggling students. Collegial and managerial cultures must rid themselves of the culture of complaint that permeates toxic cultures. This is possible if Believers begin to voice their perspectives and lobby their student-focused agendas. Fundamentalists are not shy or hesitant about lobbying. Believers can learn a lesson from this methodology. Simply closing one's door and isolating oneself from an important ideological debate is akin to sanctioning Fundamentalist beliefs. Believers need to be encouraged to lobby for extra assistance for struggling students, professional development opportunities, and changes in traditional but ineffective practices. They should feel comfortable lobbying against complaining colleagues, systems that damage students (like heavy-handed discipline and academic policies), and accepting student failure. We will explore methods to encourage Believers to do this in the next chapter.

Reversing Perceptions

Toxic school cultures are filled with drama, specifically dysfunctional interactions between professionals. These dysfunctional interactions sentence some schools to imprisonment within an atmosphere of fighting over petty issues instead of working together to achieve success for all students. Good structures, strategies, and practices do not have a chance to blossom in such an atmosphere, and toxic school cultures do not go unnoticed by the public.

One survey found that 73 percent of Americans believe teaching is an honorable profession ("73% Say Being a Teacher," 2010). This poll also found that only 24 percent of Americans think that education is a desirable career to pursue. The survey found that 60 percent of people think schools became worse in the previous twenty years, while 20 percent think schools improved in that time span. Most citizens view education and the education profession as valuable, but they also view the system as degenerating rather than improving. If educators want citizens to support public education and provide adequate political and financial support, they must work to reverse this perception.

Understanding and predicting patterns of human behavior is important in a school's quest to intentionally develop a high-will organization. The school culture framework we've described here gives us an understanding of how to positively influence the culture of a school. Believers focus their attention on the success of students and the organization as a whole, and Fundamentalists place personal goals and agendas above the collective organizational goal of educating every student. Healthy cultures cannot exist in schools dominated by Fundamentalists.

In the next chapter, we will look at how leadership at every level can impact the health of the school culture and what leaders can do specifically to create high-will schools with healthy cultures. We answer the question, Who is responsible for building a healthy school culture? Before you move on to the next chapter, reflect on the following questions.

CHAPTER 4

Reflections

1 Who dominates the agenda in your school or district, Believers or Fundamentalists? How did the dominant group gain an advantage?

2 What are the issues that bring drama to your school or district?

3 How does lobbying play out in your school or district? Who controls your staff agenda, Believers or Fundamentalists, and how do people seek advantages for their own agendas? Has this system been beneficial to your organization? If not, how can you bring attention to the situation and reframe the conversation?

4   How healthy is the communication between the collegial and managerial cultures in your school or district? Do these groups tend to be more defensive or reflective? How can you improve communication between these two groups?

5   Would you describe the professional language in your school as healthy or toxic? If it is toxic, what commitments are you willing to make to ensure that it improves?

Five

Leadership at Every Level

Who is responsible for developing a healthy school culture? Is it teachers, site or central administrators, or government officials? There are more teachers in a school than other professional staff members, so perhaps it is teachers who should lead the reform. Or maybe it is site administrators, since they have direct contact with teachers, parents, and students. But it's the central administrators who make the important policy and budget decisions that affect the most people. How about government officials who set the tone for reform and pass critical legislation?

The answer is that *all* of these groups play an important role in developing a healthy school culture. Efforts to change a school culture from low will to high will would be futile if each of these groups did not assume some responsibility in creating optimal learning environments. Leadership in a healthy school culture is a balancing act of support and accountability. Although all of these groups are important to the process, the two most essential are at the individual school level: teachers and site administrators.

Transformational Leaders

In the past, the standard response of the educational community when presented with challenges to improve was to ask for more funding and resources, and that request was usually granted. The

U.S. Department of Education (2005a) reports that when adjusted for inflation, the average expenditure per student in the United States increased from $3,400 in 1965 to $8,745 in 2001. This increase in education funding is larger than any increase since 1965, except for the military. In 2002, with the passage of No Child Left Behind, the paradigm shifted. Schools were no longer asked to improve, but they were told they must improve or lose governance and control of funding (Alloway & Runquist, 2010). Neither strategy has been effective.

If schools are to improve student performance, the school environment itself must be properly cultivated to produce the desired outcomes. Providing more funding and resources to dysfunctional, toxic environments is a waste of resources, and punishing schools that do not improve at the rate that government mandates is not effective either. Both strategies are reactionary and do not meet the needs of the modern school.

Schools need transformational leaders at every level. These leaders are determined to lead people to better behavior. They do not stop at identifying and criticizing current behavior. Rather, they actively use their influence and resources to help people improve, much like teachers do to help struggling students. These leaders have positive outlooks and believe that they can transform their schools and staff to meet their mutual goals; they emphasize communication, positive relationships, support, and accountability.

Theory X and Theory Y

Douglas McGregor's human development theory (1960) helped revolutionize the way organizations view their employees in relation to the organization's goals. McGregor's two management paradigms are Theory X and Theory Y. Theory X is based on four assumptions that a leader may hold:

1. The average person inherently dislikes work and will avoid it whenever possible.

2. Because people dislike work, they must be supervised closely, directed, coerced, or threatened with punishment

so that they put forth adequate effort toward the achievement of organizational objectives.

3. The average worker will shirk responsibility and seek formal direction from those in charge.

4. Most workers value job security above other job-related factors and have little ambition.

Theory X assumes that workers' objectives are diametrically opposed to the organization's objectives and the only way to achieve better performance is to develop systems of management that force workers to do what they would not naturally do under normal circumstances. Theory Y takes a different approach and embraces some very different assumptions:

1. If it is satisfying to them, employees will view work as natural and as acceptable as play.

2. People at work will exercise initiative, self-direction, and self-control on the job if they are committed to the objectives of the organization.

3. The average person, under proper conditions, learns not only to accept responsibility on the job, but to seek it.

4. The average employee values creativity—that is, the ability to make good decisions—and seeks opportunities to be creative at work.

Theory Y assumes that workers want to be a productive part of their work environment and, when properly cultivated, they will align their behavior with the goals and intentions of the organization. In a school environment, Theory Y is a much more desirable approach because it values high levels of autonomy and self-direction. Top-down authoritarian leadership is not an effective strategy in schools. Cultivating a community of unified professionals who work interdependently toward common goals is a much better approach.

Support Before Accountability

As Frederick Taylor (1947) noted, the ultimate goal of management is to produce organizational success. School leaders must make sure teachers have a productive environment to make success for all students a reality. The best way to cultivate such a productive environment is a system of support and nurturing, followed by accountability. Education has long lacked a healthy balance of support and accountability. Some schools are overly focused on support while others have been too focused on accountability.

The first duty of a transformational leader is to provide his or her staff with the resources necessary to achieve the desired objectives. Support must precede accountability. Accountability without support and guidance is not only ineffective, but it is unethical. It is akin to giving students a test on material that has never been taught and holding them accountable for the test results. No good teacher would do that to his or her students, and no good leader would expect results from those he or she leads without first giving them the proper resources and support. Thus, leaders must do the following three things to support their staff:

1. Clearly establish and communicate an organizational vision and direction.

2. Develop and nurture functional relationships with those that they lead.

3. Provide proper training and resources within a functional system.

4. Implement a system of accountability to monitor performance.

Table 5.1 on page 61 describes the elements of this support by transformational leaders.

These requirements of leadership provide the basic foundation for success. It is difficult for anyone to flourish in an environment with an ambiguous purpose, poor relationships, and no training opportunities, all within a dysfunctional system. To properly implement and develop these systems, Theory Y assumptions appear to be the most functional. Leaders have to believe that those they lead can accomplish organizational goals and desire to do so. This is the same approach teachers should take with their students. They must believe their students can learn before they can teach them with the techniques and rigor necessary to guarantee achievement.

Table 5.1: How Transformational Leaders Support Their Staff

Communication	• Leaders share relevant data with all stakeholders. • Leaders have thoroughly explained the rationale for change. • Leaders explore several viable alternatives for change with staff members and give staff members the opportunity to provide input and feedback.
Relationships	• Leaders make decision making a collaborative endeavor and create collaborative teams. • Leaders resolve trust issues with staff members. • Leaders ensure that change initiatives will be implemented as presented.
Support	• Leaders establish a plan for training for new initiatives. • Leaders provide a timeline for implementation. • Leaders provide resources for assisting staff members if they struggle.
Accountability	• Leaders establish a system of accountability for implementation. • Leaders establish expectations for implementation and performance that are clear and fair.

However, the Theory X paradigm also has some validity. Educators have been so focused on support from outside forces that accountability has become nonexistent. One group testing marketing material for educators found that the word *accountability* was the biggest turnoff for educators participating in a focus group (Ferrera, 2005). The validation for support should be productivity. At some point, schools and teachers must be held accountable for the education of the students they serve. When an educator is provided with all of the knowledge, skills, and resources to be successful in an environment conducive for success, the only thing left is for that educator to produce. Managing people with Theory X is valuable only after Theory Y strategies have been cultivated and effectively implemented.

Teacher Leaders

Teacher leaders play a very important role in the development of a healthy school culture. Teachers have direct contact with the clients of the educational system—the students. If the teacher culture is toxic, the chance at developing comprehensive school reform is next to impossible. The emergence of teacher leaders—especially within the collegial culture—is imperative.

What is a teacher leader? In *Awakening the Sleeping Giant: Helping Teachers Develop as Leaders* (2001), Marilyn Katzenmeyer and Gayle Moller define teacher leaders as "teachers who are leaders within and beyond the classroom, identify with and contribute to a community of teacher learners and leaders, and influence others toward improved educational practice" (p. 5). This definition paints a picture of teacher leaders as influential among peers with the goal of improving practice. Teacher leaders are guardians of a positive and healthy collegial culture.

Earlier, we established that when people become frustrated and stressed, they seek others to engage in a culture of complaint, which forms a barrier to school improvement that is difficult to penetrate. Language within the culture is emotionally charged, and colleagues use one another to vent frustration instead of solve problems. Teacher leaders can positively influence this culture. A lack of teacher leaders in the collegial culture has been a traditional weakness of school cultures (Muhammad, 2009). Believers are usually not active and influential enough in the collegial culture.

It's not hard to understand why Believers might not speak up. Group acceptance—an important human need—is one reason. Abraham Maslow (1943), in his hierarchy of needs, identifies the need to be loved by others and group identification as essential. In fact, he says they are as essential as our basic physiological and safety needs. Believers within toxic collegial cultures are faced with the choice to stand up for the principles they believe in, which often align with the administration, or try to fulfill their personal need for group identification. Many teachers fear that if they do not accept group norms, they will be ostracized from the group. We have established that the culture of complaint has no organizational value, but it may have some personal value for a teacher seeking acceptance by his or her colleagues.

To resolve this dilemma, teacher leaders determine that the needs of the students they serve are greater than their personal need to be accepted by the group. They must become what Steven Covey (1989) calls "principle centered." Someone who is *principle centered* behaves according to universal and timeless principles like justice, equity, freedom, and liberty instead of compromising his or her principles for group acceptance. Covey calls the individuals who do the latter "personality centered." Teachers must prioritize their allegiances. They must ask, "What is more important—the proper cultivation of a child or being validated by my colleagues?" When these two philosophies collide, teachers must make the decision to place students' interests before their own personal need to belong to a group. This is what makes a teacher a teacher leader.

At Jarupa Hills High School in Fontana, California, the teachers decided that they had to publicly take a stance for students. They decided to make their school a "Fundamentalist-free zone." They posted signs in several visible areas of the school proclaiming Jarupa Hills to be a student-centered environment where student development is the one and only goal of the institution. Teachers also collectively asserted disapproval for behavior that placed adult needs before student needs. They pledged to refrain from random complaints about students and parents, work together as functional teams, and communicate effectively with school administration to solve problems. They pledged to confront this behavior in both the collegial and managerial cultures. Commitments such as these must be honored and consistently implemented if a staff is to eradicate a culture of complaint. At its best, a healthy collegial culture uses its members as valuable resources for professional practice instead of trash receptacles for complaints.

Personal and Professional Development

Educators become educators because they want to successfully teach children. When they don't meet that goal, frustration is a natural result. Teachers have a choice when they are faced with this frustration: they can take an external approach and blame the student and society, or they can critically analyze their performance and seek support for their professional practice. The first method is easy, and unfortunately many teachers choose this route. The second method is more beneficial, but it is definitely the more difficult route.

One study of teacher perceptions about professional development (Webb, 1993) revealed that most teachers view professional development as an external and bureaucratic activity that generally has little value for real classroom issues. A comprehensive study of 454 teachers found that teacher attitudes about professional development are positive when the experience meets three criteria: (1) the experience is directly connected to program implementation, (2) time is allotted for implementation of learned strategies, and (3) resources are allocated to support successful implementation (Penuel, Fishman, Yamaguchi, & Gallagher, 2007). Thus, teachers find professional development valuable when it meets their needs and allows them to practice what they have learned. Professional development is most valuable when educators have input into what training they receive and how it is structured.

To share in leadership and decision making as it relates to professional development, teachers must first accept the responsibility to be a professional. A *professional* is someone with expertise in a specialized field who has not only pursued advanced knowledge to enter the field, but is also expected to remain current in the field's evolving knowledge base (DuFour & DuFour, 2006). Becoming a professional requires two commitments: a commitment to the profession and a commitment to personal growth (Muhammad, 2006/2007). These commitments require shedding the culture of complaint and making a conscious decision to become prescriptive instead of descriptive—to solve problems instead of simply talking about them.

The staff at Levey Middle School in Southfield, Michigan, decided to take personal responsibility for their students' growth and their own professional growth (Muhammad, 2008). They created what became known as "learning centers"—targeted professional development activities collaboratively created by both teachers and administrative staff. The activities were developed to fulfill the critical and immediate needs of teachers in meeting student learning requirements. Learning centers took place twice per month after school, replacing the time traditionally allotted for faculty meetings. Between 2002 and 2006, student proficiency in math and reading on state standardized assessments more than doubled.

To achieve a healthy school culture and a high-will environment, teacher leaders must emerge and become more influential in the collegial and managerial culture. In the collegial culture, Believers can influence and mold new teachers—the Tweeners—and help the Fundamentalists transform into problem solvers rather than complainers. In the managerial culture, they can ensure that administrators support the critical needs of teachers and provide professional development that gives educators the tools they need to be successful.

Site Leaders

Site leaders—principals, assistant principals, deans, and other supervisors of campus life—are the most identifiable leaders in a school. The principal is probably the most notable leader for staff members. A report on the role of the principal found that the single most influential factor in improving schools is the effectiveness of the principal (Institute for Educational Leadership, 2000). In his seven correlates of effective schools, Lawrence Lezotte (2010) puts "strong instructional leadership" at the top of his list. He writes:

> In the effective school, the principal acts as an instructional leader and effectively and persistently communicates the mission of the school to staff, parents, and students. In addition, the principal understands and applies the characteristics of instructional effectiveness in the management of the instructional program. Clearly, the role of the principal as the articulator of the mission of the school is crucial to the overall effectiveness of the school. (p. 5)

Why is site leadership so important? These leaders are the most central members of the entire organization. They have direct contact with students, teachers, parents, support staff, and central administration. If the school leader is a Fundamentalist, it can be devastating to the development of productive learning environments. If there is productivity at the site leadership level, there is hope for the development of a healthy school culture. There are three primary areas of proficiency necessary at this level:

1. Cultivating a healthy collective focus
2. Cultivating a collaborative culture
3. Cultivating accountability

Cultivating a Healthy Collective Focus

One of a school leader's first responsibilities is to cultivate a healthy common focus. He or she must develop a shared commitment to the values and practices that make a productive school environment. As we discussed earlier, educators bring their own personal ideologies and beliefs into school. This is damaging when staff members hold beliefs and values that are different than those required for success in the school, such as when they discriminate against students based on race, social class, or disability. Leaders must confront these elephants in the room because they will begin to influence policies, practices, and procedures. For example, an affluent, academically successful student might not face the same punitive attendance policies as a less-successful, struggling Latino student from a low-income home. Likewise, a school might track poor or minority students in low-level classes because educators hold stereotypes about them.

Leaders address these damaging philosophies through crucial conversations. These are discussions "between two or more people where (1) stakes are high, (2) opinions vary, and (3) emotions run strong" (Patterson, Grenny, McMillan, & Switzler, 2002, p. 3). No doubt we all agree that discussions within schools usually meet all three of these criteria. Patterson, Grenny, McMillan, and Switzler propose that during crucial conversations, leaders start with the premise that people have good intentions (Theory Y), even though we all have different philosophies. Leaders must then create a safe environment for the discussion of controversial ideas.

For example, Luis Cruz, principal of Baldwin Park High School in Baldwin Park, California, decided that his school needed to deal with the philosophical differences that had plagued the staff for years. Principal Cruz sponsored what he called a "Whine and Cheese Party." This event had three rules: (1) express whatever is on your mind, (2) no one will be judged or punished for being authentic, and (3) once an issue is aired and discussed, it is considered resolved and should not be an issue after the meeting. Staff members described the event as cleansing and transformational. They felt validated by the crucial conversation, and staff began viewing administrators as partners instead of adversaries. As we discussed in chapter 3, frustration and the anxiety that often accompanies it are natural responses to stressful situations. It is critical that leaders find productive outlets that allow their staff to become problem solvers as opposed to complainers. Principal Cruz's Whine and Cheese Party validated the staff's feelings of frustration and anxiety and helped them move beyond the frustration into collaboration. Three years later, Baldwin Park High School was presented with the prestigious California Golden Bell Award for its progress in the achievement and graduation rate of English learners.

Cultivating a Collaborative Culture

Crucial conversations require collaboration. The term *collaboration* has been made synonymous with a lot of different concepts, including collegiality and congeniality. Collaboration is neither. *Collaboration* is a "*systematic* process in which people work together, *interdependently*, to analyze and *impact* professional practice in order to improve individual and collective results" (DuFour et al., 2008, p. 464). In chapter 4 we established that collaboration is a process that requires shared commitment, proper structure, resources, and time. It is incumbent upon school leaders to support those that they lead by developing collaborative cultures.

The critical structure for a collaborative culture is the teacher team (DuFour & DuFour, 2006). In order to properly address the myriad of challenges facing schools today, such as student achievement mandates and student discipline and content and curriculum issues, educators need to work with like-minded individuals with a common goal to help them conquer their obstacles. School administrators are in the best position to carve out time for collaboration and nurture the process so that collective problem solving becomes a habit. Working within collaborative teams is the best way to prevent challenges from becoming frustrations and turn stress into satisfaction. As McLaughlin and Talbert (2006) note:

> Teacher interaction changes as teachers assume norms and collective responsibility and a service ethic, moving from questions centered on an individual teacher's competence to assessments of community capacity. When this happens, ongoing learning and critical reflection become professional norms. (p. 8)

School leaders have some power over resource allocation, schedule development, and curriculum development; teachers depend on leaders to allocate resources appropriately to best help students and to develop schedules and curricula that take into consideration student and teacher needs, and they depend on leaders to protect school resources and time. Leaders must take the stated beliefs and values of the group into consideration before designing schedules and curriculum and allocating resources—collaboration cannot become a casualty. A leader will have a very difficult time garnering universal commitment if policies, practices, resources, and procedures are incongruent with the group's goals and values. Mistakes in this area contribute to growth in the number of level-three Fundamentalists—staff members who are overloaded and lack skill and resources.

Cultivating Accountability

After leaders cultivate a supportive environment, they must be committed to accountability. Leaders who focus solely on relationships between employees can quickly forget the core purpose of their work: schools are for the education of young people, and school leaders have a responsibility to ensure that goal is met as they cultivate the environment in which that process takes place (Franken, 2010).

Once a staff has agreed on its collective commitments, the site leader is responsible for protecting those commitments and ensuring that they remain a priority. For example, if a staff makes a commitment to increase student achievement to a certain level among a subgroup of students, the site leader must lead the process by providing the necessary support for developing systems that monitor and measure student outcomes. At times, data will indicate that some staff members need assistance. Leaders must make sure staff members are held accountable—that they have the tools and assistance they require to improve their skills. Ensuring accountability sometimes means having difficult, confrontational conversations with staff members who refuse to change, and using data to support the need for change is critical in these cases (Earl & Katz, 2006). Site leaders should also celebrate the efforts of their staff when the measured results validate the success of collaborative efforts. Although most site leaders do not work directly with students in the classroom, they have a crucial responsibility in facilitating students' education by holding staff members accountable.

Central and District Leaders

Researchers have been interested in the role of central and district leaders for some time. Sheppard, Brown, and Dibbon (2008) assert that these school leaders serve three primary functions:

1. Establishing collaborative structures

2. Thinking strategically and developing adaptive learning techniques

3. Planning professional development and building capacity

Robert Marzano and Timothy Waters (2009) propose that effective school district leaders have five priorities:

1. Ensuring collaborative goal setting

2. Establishing nonnegotiable goals for achievement and instruction

3. Creating school board alignment with and support of district goals

4. Monitoring achievement and instruction goals

5. Allocating resources to support the goals for instruction and achievement

Both models establish that the role of the central office is twofold: (1) set, protect, and prioritize district goals and effective practice, and (2) cultivate and support a system for implementation of those collective goals and priorities. We do not seek to challenge these well-established principles of good central governance; rather, we want to add to the conversation by focusing on the critical cultural elements that emerge when leaders carry out these responsibilities. It is important that central office leaders recognize the impact that their behavior has on their subordinates and that they disconnect themselves from lobbies, both internal and external.

Servant Leadership

Our solar system is a network of planets that orbit around the central figure of the universe—the sun. Central administrations have traditionally been built like our universe. In his theory on scientific management, Frederick Taylor (1947) establishes top administrators as the brains of the organization and the workers as the ones to act out the will of those at the top. Administrators who adopt this outlook on leadership will not be successful.

Central administrators must remember first and foremost that the real "center of the universe" is what happens in the classroom, and their job is to support and cultivate that universe, not vice versa. The students themselves are the center, and central office leaders must always remember that they are there to serve the students. *Servant leadership*, as described by Max De Pree (1989), is based upon the notion that the highest level of leadership is servitude. He writes:

> When so much energy seems to be spent on maintenance of manuals, on bureaucracy and meaningless quantification, to be a leader is to enjoy the special privileges of complexity, of ambiguity, of diversity. But to be a leader means, especially, having the opportunity to make a meaningful difference in the lives of those who permit leaders to lead. (p. 10)

This outlook is critical to the fair implementation of policies and practices.

A Lighthouse for Ethics

Central administrators and district leaders make critical decisions that impact the lives of students, parents, and school employees, such as increasing or cutting budgets and deciding if new schools will open or existing schools will close. These leaders must make decisions through a lens of what is best for students, the community, and school staff—not what will most benefit administrators in the central office or lobbyists. When decision makers pander to special interests or act out of purely personal interest, they disappoint everyone. It is very difficult to motivate a staff that has lost confidence in its leaders.

As the popular saying goes, people will do as you do, not as you say. It is critical that leaders behave in the same way they expect their staff members to behave. This principle is important at all levels of leadership, but especially at the central office and board of education level. These leaders must recognize that they are the lighthouses for ethics. They must display the same ethical behavior they expect from others.

State and Federal Leaders

The role of the state and federal government in school culture is both direct and indirect. The government has direct impact on issues like school funding, accountability policies, and laws, but it does not have direct influence on the day-to-day operations and interactions between the members of a school society. Government leaders have the power to mandate structure, but not culture. They can pass legislation and policy, but they cannot control the implementation of that policy at the school level. Even so, like central administrators, state and federal lawmakers must consider the impact of their policy and budget decisions on the social fabric of schools. The Center on Educational Policy found that over 90 percent of teachers agreed with the goal of No Child Left Behind for universal student proficiency in math and reading, but only

38 percent of those teachers polled felt that the policy was realistic, and only 18 percent felt that the goal would ever be achieved (Jacobson, 2008). The survey shows that the vast majority of educators agree with the goal of universal achievement, but they differ in their views of how to achieve the goal. Simply mandating achievement will not make it happen. The educators polled felt that they needed financial, professional, and community support to have any chance of meeting the mandates. Obviously, a mismatch exists between the policy objectives of No Child Left Behind and what the people on the front lines—the teachers—feel is necessary to successfully achieve the goals of the policy.

We encourage lawmakers to consider carefully the social impact of their decisions. Mandating change is the worst way to actually accomplish change (Evans, 1996). Policymakers should seek out experts in school sociology and culture, economists, psychologists, and other professionals before crafting policies. No Child Left Behind and other recent policy decisions, like President Obama's Race to the Top legislation, that provide money for states willing to change policies around teacher evaluation, charter schools, and low-performing schools have affected most school cultures in a negative way because they use punishment (NCLB) and extrinsic rewards (Race to the Top) as motivational strategies. Systems of punishment and reward can lead to frustration, stress, and hopelessness, which can cause educators to have combative relationships with students and parents and result in more pronounced failure for students. In extreme cases, it can lead to unsavory behavior, such as cheating on standardized tests. In addition, these policies have made the job of future educational reform more difficult. Policymakers must be wiser when considering the effect their decisions have on practitioners and children (Brown, 2009).

Building a Healthy Culture

School culture is made up of a complex web of human interaction. As we have noted, it is more productive to analyze the roles of all members of the culture and focus on responsibility rather than blame. Again, the two most important groups in the development of healthy school cultures are teachers and site leaders. They interact the most and are closer to the students than any other professionals. Their ability to accept responsibility for successful school operation, rather than spiral into a culture of complaint, is key to healthy interaction. Although central administrators and state and federal policymakers do not have daily direct access to students, teachers, and site administrators, their role in shaping the collective agenda and allocation of resources impacts the school culture.

Any good gardener knows that it is important to develop healthy soil, but healthy soil alone cannot guarantee an abundant crop. The seeds, too, must be of high quality and cultivated to the best of the planter's ability. Like healthy soil, a healthy school culture is only the first step. A positive learning environment alone is not enough to create a high-performing school and guarantee high student academic achievement. The skills teachers possess are the high-quality seeds that make this success possible. The skill to teach must follow the will the lead. Both school culture and pedagogy must be developed around the needs of students, specifically taking into account the norms and beliefs of the school culture and students' culture—what we call a responsive pedagogy, of which students are the foundation.

Before moving on to the next part of the book—the skill section—reflect on the questions that follow.

CHAPTER 5

Reflections

1 Does your school or district operate from a Theory X or a Theory Y perspective?

2 Does support precede accountability in your school or district? How do leaders support and guide people before holding them accountable for production? Does this structure need to be improved?

3 How well do teachers and site leaders work together in your school or district? Is there more reflection or more blaming?

4 Do your central leaders act as moral and ethical lighthouses, or do they participate in politics with varying groups of internal and external lobbyists?

Six

Developing a
Responsive Pedagogy

*As to methods, there may be
a million and then some, but
principles are few. The man who
grasps principles can successfully
select his own methods.*

—Ralph Waldo Emerson

merson could have been commenting on our school system
in the United States when he wrote those words. Certainly,
in education there are a million methods, or so it seems. Principles
do often seem few and far between—especially in toxic cultures in
which educators are stressed and frustrated and leaders put policy
above student needs. As we've discussed in earlier chapters, educators in these schools do not have the will to create positive learning
environments for students—they can't achieve the skill component
because they do not yet have the will component in place. They do
not believe that all students can succeed.

We have argued that in order to achieve success for all students,
school cultures must move away from toxicity towards a healthy
state in which both staff and students flourish. We have described

what toxic and healthy school cultures look like and how the adults within these cultures feel and act. We have identified leadership as a critical issue in creating healthy school cultures—at both an administrative and a classroom level. The other component in a healthy school culture is the skill to teach. Once educators in a school have developed the will to lead, they can begin to work on the skill to teach in a way that is responsive to all students.

Simply believing in students is not enough; educators must have the skill to engage and reach students—specifically underserved and struggling students—in the classroom, and they must do so in a culturally and linguistically responsive way. Earlier in this book, we discussed many of the elements that lead school staffs to frustration. There is perhaps nothing more frustrating than a school that has the will to make changes to better serve all its students, but is unable to do so because staff lacks the skill.

What we present in this part of the book is a combination of best practices from the research and our own work with teachers in schools throughout the United States, and specifically from Sharroky's experiences at his K–8 charter school in Los Angeles, the Culture and Language Academy of Success (CLAS). Much of the content in chapters 6 through 11 of this book are centered on the instructional practices implemented at CLAS. In the pages that follow, we define and develop the parameters of a *responsive pedagogy*—a skillful and balanced framework of traditional and culturally responsive activities used within the classroom. The responsive pedagogy we present focuses on four areas of instruction we know practicing teachers must master in order to increase levels of success for all students (Marzano, 2010):

1. Classroom management

2. Academic vocabulary

3. Academic literacy

4. Learning environment

Responsive pedagogy must be coupled with a healthy culture in order to maximize the potential for success for all students, especially underserved and struggling students. Without growth in these vital instructional areas, a school's high will is irrelevant because all students will not be successful. Without a well-managed classroom, students are less likely to experience powerful learning. Students who have low academic literacy and vocabulary skills are less successful in reading/language arts as well as other school subjects. An environment that is affirming, inviting, and culturally relevant can transform a simple room or building into a place of learning where students find comfort and security.

We have developed our responsive pedagogy in this section from our more detailed and comprehensive work on culturally responsive pedagogy and from our research with African American and Latino students in particular. When researching for CLR, we realized that this approach is also beneficial with broader audiences of educators who, regardless of the demographics of their student population, desire to improve their instruction and increase student engagement. What we discovered in our research aimed initially at traditionally underserved students can play a major role in serving *all* underserved students, regardless of race, culture, language, or socioeconomic status.

Aligning the Will With the Skill

Earlier in this book, we defined *skill* as an art or a craft. This definition is important because in this section of the book, we present teaching or instruction as both an art and a science. Barrie Bennett (2010) describes effective teaching as a dynamic mixture of expertise in a vast array of instructional strategies combined with a profound understanding of individual students in class and their needs at particular points in time. In essence, to be skilled instructionally requires artfulness. Lemov (2010) says that great art relies on the mastery and application of foundation skills, learned individually through diligent study. This is how we examine the skill of teaching in this section. Specifically, within the skill, there is an art to the teaching. They are not mutually exclusive, and to a certain extent they are one and the same. In fact, Piestrup (1973) asserts that responsive teaching *is* artful teaching.

In this book, we cannot cover *all* of the most effective instructional skills teachers need to gain better academic results. There is no shortage of research on what works instructionally and what the most effective teaching techniques are. For example, in his work, Robert Marzano (2009a) provides what he considers to be the forty-one most high-yield strategies for effective teaching. Other respected researchers, such as Grant Wiggins, David Berliner, and Carol Ann Tomlinson, to name a few, provide guidance on effective teaching (Marzano, 2010). Doug Lemov (2010) promotes forty-nine instructional techniques that put students on the path to college in his book *Teach Like a Champion*. The New America Foundation (2008) notes that many programs appear to work; for example, Wade Carpenter (2000) counted 361 "good ideas" that appeared during a ten-year period in education. We could go on for several pages listing the litany of books, articles, and reports on successful teaching techniques. These researchers and others do a notable job of updating the knowledge base regarding effective teaching and providing clear suggestions about how instruction can improve.

In our work with teachers and students throughout the United States, particularly in urban areas with populations of students who have typically been underserved, we have found that teachers do know about effective techniques—they have the tools. What many teachers lack is the understanding of how to use these strategies with their students, along with the knowledge that they can have success. In short, educators don't necessarily need *just* more effective techniques. Rather, they need to understand how to use those techniques skillfully and artfully. We propose that educators need to take the myriad of recommendations and prescriptions for effective teaching and use them responsively to benefit first students who are not having success and ultimately all students. The goal is that every teacher uses responsive instruction in the four critical areas we explore here. We provide sample activities to illustrate the strategies that we feel are critical within a responsive classroom. These activities are used at CLAS and have been shown to be effective there. Teachers are encouraged, however, to use a variety of activities responsively within the focus areas we emphasize and in other instructional areas that they identify within their personal professional practice.

Skill *Is* Being Responsive

Before moving forward, we want to define specifically what we mean by a responsive pedagogy. *Pedagogy* is a word frequently used in academic circles. It is broadly defined as a method and practice of teaching, especially as an academic subject or a theoretical concept. We define it as the *how* and *why* of teaching, the strategic use of methods and techniques, and the rationale behind why decisions are made instructionally to best serve the students who are in the most need (Hollie, 2011). We define *responsive pedagogy* in the following way:

> The validation and affirmation of the home cultural and linguistic behaviors of the students through selected instructional practices for the purposes of building and bridging the student to increased success in the cultural and linguistic demands of academia (school) and mainstream society. Put another way, a responsive pedagogy is going to where the students are culturally and linguistically for the aim of bringing them where they need to be academically. (Hollie, 2011, p. 21)

Compared to a traditional pedagogy, which by default is one size fits all, a responsive pedagogy is differentiated instruction. Whereas traditional pedagogy is typically a one-way interaction and teacher directed, responsive pedagogy is steeped in two-way interactions and tends to be student directed. However, although we nudge educators to move toward a more responsive pedagogy, it is not at the exclusion of traditional pedagogy. The challenge teachers face, and the skill they must acquire, is knowing when to validate and affirm students—when to be responsive instructionally—and when to use traditional instruction.

We turn now, therefore, to the acquisition of the skill and the art of knowing when to be responsive and how educators can use a responsive pedagogy optimally—as individual instructional practitioners, as learning communities, as schools, or as organizations—to ultimately improve student success.

Three Lessons From Hollywood

A great illustration of how a responsive pedagogy can work is in the film *Mr. Holland's Opus* (Cort, Field, Nolin, & Herek, 1995). In a critical scene, the main character, Mr. Holland, played by Richard Dreyfuss, realizes what it really means to be a teacher—a *responsive* teacher. His best friend, the varsity football coach, asks him to take one of his star football players into his band class. The coach figures band will be an easy class for the student to pass, therefore keeping him eligible for the team. The student is very motivated; however, he does poorly in the class. During a friendly game of chess, Mr. Holland tells his colleague the bad news: the coach's star football player is not going to pass the class.

The coach, astonished and disappointed, looks Mr. Holland in the eyes and, in not so many kind words, questions his ability to teach. He tells Mr. Holland if he cannot teach this kid who is motivated and really wants to learn, then he cannot teach at all. Mr. Holland is devastated by his friend's harsh words, but he realizes that, while inspiring to his students, he has not been teaching responsively to the level necessary to move students from one proficiency level to the next.

In the film, the football player has to learn how to play the drums with rhythm. To his credit, rather than give up, Mr. Holland—in pure Hollywood form, background music and all—steps up and shows his ability to be responsive to meet the need of the student. He uses effective, validating, and affirming techniques to support the student, including one-to-one teaching, building background knowledge, scaffolding, total physical response, modeling, and plenty of praise, to name a few. The final scene shows the student accomplishing the goal of playing his drums on beat.

Skill Recognition, Activation, and Application

There are three main lessons in this fictional scene that help us learn how to develop the skill to be responsive in our teaching. Lesson one is *recognition through collaboration*. Mr. Holland is not a bad teacher by any means. In fact, generally speaking, he would be considered an average to good teacher in terms of his ability to inspire students, work ethic, level of content knowledge, and rapport with students. What he learns, though, is that he has not been the best teacher to *all* his students—specifically his struggling and underachieving students—and that he can do better. He recognizes his lack of skill application through an impromptu collaboration with a colleague. This lesson is supported by what we emphasized earlier in the will section of this book—the importance of developing a collaborative culture as a critical feature of a healthy school culture.

The second lesson is *activity through stratagem*. Put another way, Mr. Holland pulls from a bevy of resources to begin to teach the student in an effective manner. Previously, he has used what we call the "say it louder and slower" approach—or, at best, traditional approaches. After he realizes that his teaching is falling short, though, he pulls from his strategy tool belt to use the most effective activities for the struggling student. The key point is he has the activities in his tool belt, albeit latent, to move the student—he just needs to activate them in an intentional, purposeful, and strategic way. He needs to be responsive to the student.

The third lesson from the movie is *success through application*. Simply, Mr. Holland applies the skills successfully. Many teachers apply the skills or strategies, but do so without improving results. Recognizing what is needed or that there is a problem with one's teaching and then using a set of skills intended to address the problem are necessary steps, but they are not sufficient. If a teacher cannot implement responsive activities successfully, then the goal of increasing student engagement is not accomplished. Mr. Holland is able to accomplish his goal by successfully applying the responsive activities.

Many teachers we work with across the United States are able to apply responsive activities, but they do so unevenly. Simply *doing* an activity is not enough; educators must use them with success. This connects to the idea of a need for a high-will culture put forth earlier in the book. It is vital to have the will to continue trying, even when the immediate results are not exactly what we expect.

In Hollywood, there is almost always a happy ending to the story. The question for real-life teachers is, How can we garner more happy endings using the lessons from *Mr. Holland's Opus*?

Recognizing the Need for a Responsive Pedagogy

Before we can enact a responsive pedagogy, we must be able to simply recognize that there is a need for it in the first place. At its most optimistic, analysis of achievement levels in American schools sees the glass as half full, as critics such as Diane Ravitch (2010) note. Even at half full, when it comes to most indicators, we must consider the system a collective failure. Put bluntly, the glass needs to be completely full, and looking at just one factor—high school graduation rates—demonstrates why this must be so. One third of all students fail to graduate in the United States, and only one half of African American, Latino, and Native American students graduate on time from high school (New America Foundation, 2008). One report showed that in some urban communities nearly 60 percent of African American males are failing to graduate from high school (National Association for the Advancement of Colored People, 2011). With numbers like these, few would argue that we need to do better and do differently.

As we have moved into the second decade of the 21st century, the spotlight has been on the quality of teaching. The notion of value-added teaching—determining teachers' pay based on student achievement scores—is at the forefront, along with awards and sanctions for schools or districts that improve or fail. We believe that all teachers, effective or ineffective, should commit to improving their practice or skill level. We assume that there is always a need to improve. We could look at almost any school data and find the need to do something different. Recognizing the need for change requires reflection, but rarely in the laundry list of what to improve upon or what techniques to use for improvement is there a prescription for *how to reflect*. It is left up to chance, like what happens to Mr. Holland with his friend during a game of chess.

If we are to improve results, we must reflect more intensely and deeply. As we noted earlier, we recommend asking the following critical questions (DuFour et al., 2008):

1. What do we want students to learn?

2. How will we know if students have learned it?

3. How will we respond when students have not learned?

Teachers must know the learning intentions and success criteria, and when the goals are not met, there has to be reflection and discussion around instructional needs (Hattie, 2009).

Identifying the Audience for Responsive Pedagogy

A responsive pedagogy most benefits *any* student who is underserved. An *underserved student* is any student who is not successful academically, socially, and/or behaviorally in school because the school as an institution is not being responsive to the student (Hollie, 2011). We intentionally use the term *underserved* rather than common terms such as *underachieving* and *underperforming*. These terms imply deficits within the students themselves and put the onus on students, whereas the term *underserved* is based on the premise that students are clients who are not being served adequately by the school. In other words, the school as an institution is failing the student. Underserved students are a broad category, and that is the point.

Think for a moment about which students in your school you would identify as underserved; you are probably thinking about students of different races, cultures, and languages, or special needs students, including the gifted. What if you asked all the underserved students you have identified to come to the gymnasium? What would the group look like? The research (Ogbu, 1978, 2003) tells us who these students are most likely to be: African Americans, Mexican Americans, Native Americans, Samoan Americans, and/or Eastern Asian Americans and immigrants. The overall intention is to better serve *all* students, but when we look at who is in the gymnasium, we find these students to be of color primarily. When considering the group of underserved students, we understand why a responsive pedagogy is important: the educational reform movements of the 21st century have been conceptualized and implemented because of the system's chronic failure with these students. These students will best benefit from a responsive pedagogy because of its validating and affirming activities that engage students and build a bridge from students' existing cultural knowledge to the academic knowledge they must master.

Beware of Deficit Thinking

As we have suggested throughout this book, when it comes to underserved students, many educators' beliefs and attitudes tend to be deficit oriented. In other words, they focus on students' shortcomings and blame students for their failures—students become the problem. The mindset of the deficit-oriented educator is quite simply, "If we had better students, then we would have better schools," or "Our scores were good until *those students* started coming here," or "Everyone in our school seems to be doing well except for *those students*." Students are viewed as lacking something. Underserved students are many times seen as deficient, deviant, defiant, disruptive, and disrespectful. What they bring to the classroom culturally and linguistically is seen not as an asset, but rather as a liability. Therefore, teachers are "off the hook"—since they can blame students for their own failure, there is no need to develop a responsive pedagogy. In a healthy school culture, educators have high will when it comes to student learning. When their culture is also high skill, they do what they must do to make student success a reality. They acquire the appropriate tools to become responsive in their instructional approach. Developing and using a responsive pedagogy is the opposite of deficit thinking for educators—it supports the mindset that all students can succeed.

Becoming Skillful

In this chapter, we've examined teaching as both an art and a science. We have discussed how educators need to consider the voluminous research on effective teaching techniques and utilize it responsively. We have defined the term *responsive pedagogy*, talked about why it is needed, and revealed that acquiring such a pedagogy is a three-step process of recognition, activation, and application. Finally, we discussed the need for responsive pedagogy for our underserved student population specifically, though all students benefit.

In the next chapter, we explain the steps to developing a responsive pedagogy. Before you move on to the next chapter, reflect on the questions that follow.

CHAPTER 6

Reflections

1 Who are the underserved students in your school or district and therefore the students who will most benefit from a responsive pedagogy?

2 What is your school or district's current approach to underserved students?

3 Where is responsive pedagogy currently occurring at your school or district, if at all?

4 What types of opportunities are there for collaborative, reflective discussions about instruction at your school or district?

Seven

The Steps to a Responsive Pedagogy

uring a recent broadcast of a National Basketball Association (NBA) game, the broadcaster referred to one of the participants in the game as an "athlete, but not a basketball player." What did the broadcaster mean by this? He meant that as a player, the participant had great athletic skills—speed, strength, agility, and coordination. However, as those skills applied to the specifics of basketball playing, the player was not as great. He did not possess the knowledge base, the experience, or the nuances necessary for playing like a seasoned basketball player.

This example from sports provides another way of looking at the difference between having a general skill set as a teacher and being a responsive educator. The athlete in the basketball game had enough skills to be good; however, he lacked the ability to play basketball greatly. Similarly, many teachers have a skill set or access to skills (the tools in their belts), but they lack the pedagogy to bring forth the desired outcomes, particularly with struggling students (Bennett, 2010). Some teachers are strong in the how of teaching (the methodology), but they are weak in the what (the content); others are strong in content, but they are weak in their methodology. Strong pedagogy finds a balance between the how and the what of teaching. Many teachers would claim that what they teach (the content) is mandated and non-negotiable (and how they are measured is mandated and non-negotiable, as well), but how they teach (their methodology) is left up to them and their professional judgment. Teachers can develop the skill to choose responsive methodology.

Methodology has two parts: strategy and activity. *Strategy* is the plan or the method. The *activity* is the actual event that carries out the strategy. For example, using attention signals is a strategy for classroom management. Teachers can choose from many activities to implement this strategy. Most teachers choose a traditional approach, such as turning the light on and off to get students' attention. We advocate that teachers choose a responsive approach, such as a "call and response activity" (explained in more detail in chapter 8) that engages students, validates them in some way, and also succeeds in the overall goal of the strategy—to bring students to attention or to indicate a transition. The use of strategies and activities can be summed up with a chess metaphor: skilled players come to a match with a strategy in mind, a game plan, and a pattern of attack, and then they choose which pieces they want to play to engage their strategy—they don't just move their pieces around the board randomly.

Now we will walk through a three-step process for developing a responsive pedagogy. This process involves (1) identifying an area of instruction for improvement, (2) assessing the quantity and quality of current activities, and (3) implementing responsive activities during teaching.

Step One: Indentify an Area of Instruction for Improvement

There are many instructional areas in which teachers can further develop their skills by using responsive activities. The areas teachers choose no doubt depend on their content-area focus, the grade level they teach, and their student population, to name a few variables. We encourage teachers to take the first step of developing a responsive pedagogy by identifying an area of instruction to assess and then infusing responsive activities. For the purposes of this book, we identify four broad areas of instruction that we think of as "school staples"—areas in which all teachers in all classrooms, regardless of grade level or content area, should strive to implement responsive best practices both effectively and efficiently. These four areas include (1) classroom management, (2) academic vocabulary, (3) academic literacy, and (4) learning environment. We believe teachers should focus on their specific skills within those instructional areas when developing a responsive pedagogy. To be clear, the first step in developing a responsive pedagogy is for teachers to identify any area of instruction in which they desire to improve and then continue with the steps to develop their specific skills within that area. In this book, we have chosen to focus on four critical areas and specific skills within them that we believe are most critical for teachers of underserved students and then to describe what a responsive pedagogy might look like in these areas.

Responsive Classroom Management

In responsive classroom management, the teacher facilitates the collaborative process, and the students participate in it. Responsive management is inclusive and student centered, and it incorporates elements of students' culture, home, and community to engage them more deeply in the learning process. We believe there are three specific classroom management strategies that teachers must implement responsively in order to have success overall and particularly with underserved students: (1) using effective discussing and responding techniques, (2) using effective attention-getting signals, and (3) integrating movement activities into instruction. Effective responding and discussing techniques (for example, the random selection activities teachers use to call on students) establish a learning environment in which everyone plays a critical role and is validated in the process. Effective attention signals bring students back to task after group discussions and during transitions. For example, rather than using a traditional attention signal, such as a hand raised in the air, a teacher might decide to use a call-and-response activity wherein she calls out a phrase or word and the students respond. The third strategy, creating structured activities for movement to occur in the classroom, enhances student learning.

In chapter 8, we examine responsive classroom management more deeply and provide suggestions for specific responsive activities within this instructional area.

Responsive Academic Vocabulary

Responsive academic vocabulary instruction builds on the word knowledge students bring with them to school—the words students "own." Many of these words come from students' cultural backgrounds, their homes, and their communities. These words are abstractly connected to academic vocabulary; students have an understanding of these words that is connected to their own usage, not to the specific academic meaning of the words. Strategies and activities within responsive vocabulary instruction bridge students' knowledge of their own words and expand this knowledge to the academic vocabulary. For example, a student might understand the concept of the word *thirsty*. Through responsive vocabulary instruction, a teacher can build on the student's concept of *thirsty* and bridge his use of the word to the more academic term *parched*. A responsive pedagogy in this area includes effective common vocabulary strategies, such as wide and abundant reading, contextualization and conceptualization of words, knowledge of word parts, and synonym development. Teachers can build on students' word knowledge using a tool called the Personal Thesaurus and by focusing on content-specific words through the use of another tool, the Personal Dictionary (Hollie, 2011).

In chapter 9, we examine responsive academic vocabulary more deeply and provide suggestions for specific responsive activities within this instructional area.

Responsive Academic Literacy

The next instructional area we have identified is responsive academic literacy: using text, fiction, and nonfiction to validate and affirm culture and language. Strong literacy skills in reading, writing, speaking, and listening are critical for student success in most content areas. Students who are strong readers and writers tend to be strong in other subjects, such as math, science, and social studies

(August & Shanahan, 2006). Think about it. As a teacher, do you often have students who are enrolled in a basic reading class and at the same time enrolled in algebra II? The answer is generally no. Thus, teachers' responsive use of text in instruction is very important.

In this instructional area, to become responsive, we recommend that practitioners artfully and skillfully use read-alouds as a form of storytelling to better engage students (Trelease, 2001). We also promote using strategic supplemental text selections in addition to the core text on a regular basis. A science teacher, for example, while using the state-mandated textbook, would also include articles, stories, and facts to supplement the standards-based topics covered in the book. The purpose of this supplementing is to add a perspective that might be more relevant to students' lives. Finally, we encourage the use of engaging literacy strategies, many of which are connected to oral and written language development and beneficial to struggling readers and writers alike.

In chapter 10, we examine responsive academic literacy more deeply and provide suggestions for specific responsive activities within this instructional area.

Responsive Learning Environment

A responsive learning environment is an important aspect of the overall pedagogy. Of particular importance is an environment that reflects the cultures and backgrounds of students. The school environment can influence student behavior, so how school spaces are organized (with regular "cemetery rows" of seats versus learning centers, for example) and what they contain (a wide variety of culturally relevant materials as opposed to strictly traditional academic materials, for example) can have a profound impact on student achievement by sending strong messages that encourage students to act in particular ways. All students thrive in language-rich environments rife with symbols and print. These environments stimulate language development and literacy acquisition. They create the context in which movement and learning activities take place. Also, the classroom environment must provide resources and instructional materials that are high interest to underserved students and engage them in the learning process.

In chapter 11, we examine responsive learning environments more deeply and provide suggestions for specific responsive elements and activities within this instructional area.

Step Two: Assess the Quantity and Quality of the Activities Currently Used

As we've mentioned before, many teachers already use strategies and activities recommended in the research—they have the tools in their tool belts—they are just not applying them responsively. Step two of the process for developing a responsive pedagogy, therefore, involves a quick reflection on the strategies and activities already in use—*the quantity.* If the strategies and activities are already in place, then the next question is, Are they working successfully? This is what we call *the quality.* The purpose of this step is for teachers to gauge what is working in terms of teaching and learning in their classrooms and what is not. If current traditional strategies and activities are not working, then teachers must decide to do something different, such as infusing responsive strategies and activities into their instruction. An example from responsive classroom management will help illustrate this step.

First, a teacher determines that he should use activities for movement in his classroom. (We agree with this determination, as we have identified effective movement activities as one component of responsive classroom management, as noted earlier.) According to brain-based research, movement in the classroom is positive and necessary to assist learning (Jensen, 2003, 2005). Allowing students to move around the room while involved in structured instructional conversations provides a different way of learning to which many students respond positively. Many of the teachers with whom we work, particularly those who work with underserved students, do not often use activities that involve movement because they do not believe they will be able to get their students back on task. We recommend to educators that elementary students should be moving at least two to three times per hour and secondary students one to two times per hour. Once a teacher establishes the rationale for using a particular strategy, such as using effective movement activities, then it is time to check for quantity of use during instruction (Hollie, 2011).

To continue the example of movement, a teacher would ask himself, "How many times do my students move in a class period, on average?" This depends on the grade level, of course. Hopefully, the answer is that the teacher uses the frequency prescribed by the research. If this is not the case, then a change must occur so the teacher is more responsive to his students. After establishing the quantity, the teacher would then check for quality.

If students are moving two to three times per hour, what activities are they doing, and, most important, are the activities working? For example, in one of our trainings, a teacher offered a question-answer relay game as an example of a movement activity. He used the game to review for a test. The students approached the board, and the teacher gave them a question. If the students gave the correct answer, they could then relay the answer to a teammate, and the teammate would approach the board. While the students were moving, the quality of this movement was not constructive. Simply having one student move to the front of the room to answer questions is not considered quality instructional movement. In effective instructional movement activities, all students are moving, and they are all involved in instructional conversations while moving. Teachers can also incorporate culturally responsive elements into these activities to further engage students. This makes the movement of higher quality. (In chapter 8, we suggest some examples of specific movement activities that fit into a responsive pedagogy.)

Step Three: Implement Responsive Activities During Teaching

The final step in the process of developing a responsive pedagogy is implementing responsive activities and techniques skillfully during instruction. The central question teachers should ask themselves in this step is, "What makes my teaching skillful? What specific activities and techniques can I use in the general lesson to increase engagement and relate to students?" Continuing the example of the movement activity the teacher shared earlier, the first way a teacher can make it more engaging is by including four steps that would add more structure, purpose, and responsiveness (Hollie, 2011):

1. The teacher can get all students moving. Unless students have physical limitations or challenges, the expectation is that everyone will be out of their seats—not just one student to write on the board.

2. The teacher can require students to greet one another before they share the review information with each other. This greeting can come through a particular cultural orientation that has been learned in students' homes or communities. For example, in Black culture, students might greet one another with a "soul shake" or the "Black man's hug." Students from a Middle Eastern culture might greet using a cheek kiss. Students from every background use greetings that are unique to their families or communities.

3. The teacher can use another activity, such as Give One, Get One (Kagan & Kagan, 2009), to add quality. In this example, students give a response (give one) to the classmate who is sharing information with them (get one).

4. The teacher can instruct students not to talk with certain students, such as those in their row or group or the group or row to the right or left of them. The purpose is to increase interactivity among students, rather than allowing them to continue talking to the same students (usually those sitting around them or in their group).

These four activities then become part of the teacher's responsive pedagogy for using effective movement activities. Every time students move, they are to utilize these steps, which increase their engagement and add elements of cultural relevance to their academic learning.

The Art of Juxtapositions

An *instructional juxtaposition* is when a responsive activity, such as those described in the movement example in step three and later in the book in chapters 8 through 11, is paired with a traditional activity (Hollie, 2011). Traditional strategies are typically teacher centered, provide medium-to-high affective filters (are high anxiety for students), limit student choice, and involve what we call "random urgency"—teachers calling on students at any time and students not resisting because they believe the process is fair and random.

A simple example of an instructional juxtaposition combines a responsive activity called Shout Out with a traditional activity called Back It Up. The teacher gives the class a question, and first, students are allowed to spontaneously give their responses verbally. They can "shout out" their responses, but their responses have to be in one word and/or called out in unison in most cases. For instance, a teacher might ask, "What is the answer for the problem 2×3?" The teacher would then say, "Shout out!" and the class would respond with "Six!" Then, the teacher would follow up by asking a student to volunteer to explain why $2 \times 3 = 6$. The responsive activity Shout Out allows for spontaneity, lowered affective filter (less anxiety), and choral response. The teacher pairs it with a traditional activity we call Back It Up in which the teacher asks a question to the entire class and then asks students to raise their hands to respond. When called upon, a student will provide the answer and then "back it up" with more explanation. So, in this example, the teacher juxtaposed Shout Out to Back It Up as a means to first engage the students and then go deeper in the lesson.

We strongly encourage teachers to use instructional juxtapositions frequently within a responsive pedagogy. A series of these types of juxtapositions can be empowering, not only for students, but for teachers as well. One teacher made the following comment after using juxtapositions in her teaching: "When I give activities that are responsive to my students, I seem to get more out of it than they do. It is liberating. It is empowering." These juxtapositions allow us to see how responsive pedagogy provides leverage for the instruction—they give teachers options and allow them to plan activities that will fully engage their unique students. Teachers feel empowered because they have the capacity to create dynamic lessons that directly meet the needs of their students and liberated from sometimes restrictive traditional approaches.

Steps for Success

In this chapter we have presented three steps for developing a responsive pedagogy. Teachers begin by identifying an instructional area to improve; we have identified four broad areas—classroom management, academic vocabulary, academic literacy, and learning environment—that we believe are critical in a responsive pedagogy. Then, educators must assess the quantity and quality of their instructional techniques in these areas. Very simply, do they exist, to what frequency or depth do they exist, and are they working successfully? The last step is to infuse specific responsive activities into the instruction, while at the same time trying to create instructional juxtapositions with traditional activities.

In the next chapter, we begin our examination of those specific responsive activities teachers can infuse in the third step. Chapter 8 explores specific activities within the first area—responsive classroom management. Before you move to the next chapter, reflect on the questions that follow.

CHAPTER 7

Reflections

1 In which of the four broad educational areas is responsive pedagogy most needed in your district, school, or classroom?

2 In which of these areas should your school begin? Why?

3 How would you describe the instruction in general in your district, school, or classroom—more traditional or more responsive?

4 What professional development opportunities do you have available to you so that you or the teachers in your district or school can put more tools into your tool belts?

Eight

Responsive Classroom Management

While the adage that an engaging lesson plan is the best classroom management plan is true, the need for an effective, positive classroom management system always exists (Marzano, Marzano, & Pickering, 2003). In general, effective classroom management means that instruction can occur without interruptions and disruptions, that students feel safe and comfortable to take risks and to approximate or make mistakes, and that the environment is conducive to optimal learning (Kohn, 1996). To be clear, there is no shortage of strategies and activities for classroom management. What we propose here (and in the chapters that follow for the other instructional areas) is not *prescriptive*; rather, we intend it to be descriptive—to show what responsive instruction looks like. It is our hope that teachers will use the three-step process described in the previous chapter to identify need, assess current practices, and ultimately choose a wide variety of responsive activities to implement in their classrooms.

Before we explore responsive activities in classroom management, it is necessary to discuss philosophies within this instructional area.

Philosophies of Classroom Management

When choosing strategies and activities for classroom management, teachers must first be knowledgeable about the general philosophies of classroom management. They must consider which philosophy they aspire to and which one they actually practice (Emmer, Everston, & Worsham, 2003). The three most common philosophies of classroom management are (1) authoritarian, (2) permissive, and (3) democratic, which is sometimes called collaborative. *Authoritarian* management is the most traditional type. In this style, primary control of the classroom rests with the teacher. The teacher is in charge—literally. *Permissive* management is on the opposite end of the spectrum. With this style, students are not only in control, but they are in control in a way that can be negative and confrontational, causing anxiety in the environment. In general, students do not like these types of classrooms, and administrators should not tolerate them. The philosophy that best aligns with developing a responsive pedagogy is the democratic or collaborative style (Kohn, 1996).

Democratic management is a collaborative process in which teacher and students co-create a safe, comfortable environment that is conducive to learning. The teacher facilitates the collaborative process, and the students participate in it. The democratic approach can be the most effective because teachers have control of the classroom while students develop a love of learning. The democratic approach fits with a responsive pedagogy because it is inclusive and student centered, it involves student choice, and it is reflective and collaborative. These characteristics support students by engaging them more deeply in the learning process. The democratic approach involves both the art and the science of teaching, meshing intuition and skill. Often, the art aspect in this type of management cannot be taught traditionally. Rather, it tends to evolve through experience and direct guidance from mentors. Students respond more positively to the democratic approach when there is an established respect for the teacher, an understood rapport between the student and the teacher, and a developing, bonding relationship—what we call the "three Rs" (Hollie, 2011).

The Three P Approach

The Three P Approach to classroom management (Hollie, 2011, based on Emmer et al., 2003) identifies three critical elements of classroom management within a responsive pedagogy. It calls for classroom management that is (1) positive, (2) proactive, and (3) preventative.

The first P, being positive, is the most significant of the three within a responsive approach to pedagogy. Being positive means recognizing and appreciating students—especially underserved students. It means having a positive vibe and energy, and consistently demonstrating a set of often intangible characteristics such as care, empathy, sensitivity, kindness, calmness, humor, forgiveness, and patience (Gay, 2000). Being positive means not allowing student behavior to make you feel negative, finding joy in work, and having the spark that matters so much in teaching. Teachers can best show their positivity with affirmations—positive sayings, poems, verses, and words of praise (Gay, 2000).

The second P, being proactive, means always looking ahead. Responsive pedagogy demands predicting potential problems and knowing where trouble can arise. The opposite is reactivity—when teachers wait for students to act out and then respond. For example, if a fight occurs during recess, when students return to the classroom, some will clearly be upset about it, and their emotion will carry over into class. The proactive teacher addresses the episode and emotions immediately, while the reactive teacher sits back and allows something to occur in the class as a result of the incident. Being proactive means really knowing students. This includes recognizing when situations outside of school might affect what happens in the classroom. Without proactivity, teachers lose control of the classroom and spend their time putting out fires instead of focusing on instruction.

The final P is prevention. In classroom management, prevention often means choosing your battles. An educator decides to either battle with a student in an ongoing manner or deal with the problem in a way that sends the message to the student that his or her behavior is unacceptable but does not drain time and energy away from instruction. In most cases, teachers can prevent problems with changes in the classroom environment (Emmer et al., 2003).

For example, suppose a teacher wants students to enter through one door and exit through another door. One student refuses to do so and enters and exits out of both doors. The preventative teacher simply locks one door when he wants students to enter the other way, and locks the other door when he wants students to exit. Another example is when a teacher is faced with a student who she thinks is stealing from her desk. Rather than watching the student constantly, the teacher simply clears her desk of anything that can be stolen. Using prevention saves time in the long run because teachers are not constantly battling with students.

Figure 8.1 highlights the elements of a responsive classroom-management system where the three Ps are paramount and the teacher has a democratic philosophy.

---

1. My students respect me. They have confidence they will learn in my class.

2. I feel comfortable that I can communicate with my students in multiple ways and that they "get me."

3. I know my students, their personalities, where they are from, their family history, what makes them tick and thrive, and what sets them off.

4. In general, I have a positive, affirming, caring classroom energy and vibe.

5. Most times, I am proactive with students who could show troublesome behavior.

6. My classroom is arranged in a way that prevents potential classroom management problems.

7. My classroom management philosophy is collaborative and democratic, but authoritarian when necessary.

Figure 8.1: Elements of a responsive classroom-management system built on the Three Ps.

Activities for Responsive Classroom Management

In the following sections, we describe specific strategies for responsive classroom management within three focus areas:

1. Discussing and responding techniques

2. Attention signals

3. Movement activities

We focus on these three areas within classroom management because we believe they are critical to teacher and student success.

Effective Discussing and Responding Techniques

Consider how many times a day your whole class is engaged in responding to prompts or questions. During these times, you already have an expectation of how you want students to participate with you, whether they are simply listening, silently taking an assessment, answering questions individually, or shouting out an answer in unison. In a responsive classroom, there is never a time during instruction when students are not participating, whether they are responding as a whole group or discussing in small groups.

Giving students multiple ways of discussing and responding in class is part of a responsive pedagogy because it increases student engagement and decreases classroom management issues (Kagan & Kagan, 2009). The key is making the structures for responding and discussing explicit so that students will know exactly how to respond in class and how to conduct discussions and why. In other words, the teacher knows the purpose of the question he or she is asking (checking for understanding, assessing prior knowledge, checking for engagement, volunteering personal experiences, and so on) and clearly communicates how he or she wants students to respond. This teaches students *situational appropriateness*—what types of cultural and linguistic behaviors and participation are appropriate in different situations (Hollie, 2011). This is a critical skill many underserved students must master. In addition, consistently using different types of response and discussion techniques in the classroom leads to increased student participation overall.

Nonvolunteer forms of responding—random selection—encourage accountability and engagement on the part of learners, as well as provide more accurate feedback to the teacher about student understanding while in whole-group situations. Random-selection activities communicate to students not only that their attention and participation during whole-group instruction and questioning is required for them as learners, but also that they are all integral members of the classroom community, and everybody's thoughts and ideas are necessary for an effective learning environment.

The Pick-a-Stick activity is one example of a random-selection response activity. In this activity, the teacher poses a question, and then students think about the answer silently. After sufficient thought time, the teacher picks from a group of sticks representing each student. The chosen student answers the question. Stick selection can continue until the class hears a sufficient number of answers. Another example is Roll 'Em. In this activity, students are seated in groups of four to six. They think about a posed question as the teacher rolls two dice: one that represents the table or group number and one that represents the seat number. The student sitting in the seat represented by the rolled dice answers the question. Rolling of the dice continues until the class hears a sufficient number of answers.

Pick-a-Stick and Roll 'Em randomly sample students to assess prior knowledge and understanding, but unlike the traditional activity of simply calling on students, they maintain whole-group engagement within the direct instruction, thus reducing the number of students who are off task or not paying attention. Importantly, they hold students accountable for participation.

Structured discussion activities also serve to further engage students in the learning, keeping them on task. In Roundtable, a discussion activity, teachers organize students into teams of three or four students who then respond to a question or problem by stating their ideas aloud as each member writes them on a single sheet of paper. The paper is then passed around the table until time is called. As students vocalize their ideas as they write, other students can reflect on them. This activity encourages all students to contribute their ideas and participate in a group, and keeps them engaged during the group work.

To be most effective in their classroom management, teachers should use varied activities such as these for structured responding and discussing throughout the entire day or class period. Table 8.1 summarizes successful activities and techniques used at CLAS in grades K through 8 and in our work with hundreds of schools across the United States. (For a longer list of responsive activities, see Hollie, 2011.)

Table 8.1: Examples of Effective Discussing and Responding Activities for Responsive Classroom Management

Shout Out
Students softly shout out responses in unison. The teacher can record shout-outs on the board, if appropriate. Questions can require either one correct answer or a variety of short answers.
This activity actively engages all students and validates and affirms cuturally different forms of discourse.

Train or Pass It On
Students call on each other to answer and/or ask questions. Students should not raise their hands to be called on, and they should be encouraged to call on a variety of people in the classroom. Students can also pass on a question (pass it on) if they do not want to answer by calling on another student for help. This can be done with the use of a small, soft object that students can toss to one another in order to pass it on.
This activity holds all students accountable for participation, validates and affirms culturally different forms of discourse, provides students with variety and opportunities to improvise, and allows students to control participation.

Raise a Righteous Hand
Students raise a hand or fist to volunteer information that is specific to their experiences.
This activity gives students practice in explicit turn taking.

Whip Around
Each student in the room takes a turn responding to a posed question with quick answers. Teachers use seating order (or another easy-to-follow order) to avoid having to constantly facilitate which student answers next. Responses should come very quickly, so the question must be precise.
This activity gives students practice with explicit turn taking, validates everyone's responses, and allows for precise, focused responding.

(continued ➡)

Numbered Heads Together

The teacher puts students in groups of four to six students, numbering each student within each group. When asked a question, students work together in their groups to find the best answer. When called together again, the teacher rolls a die and asks the students from all groups whose number was rolled (for example, all threes from each group) to stand. Each student then reports his or her group's answer.

This activity helps to form a consensus and encourage accountability.

Think, Pair, Share

This involves a three-step cooperative structure. During the first step, students think silently about a question posed by the teacher. Individuals then pair up during the second step and exchange thoughts. In the third step, the pairs share their responses with other pairs or the entire group. It is usually a good idea for individuals asked to share with the whole group to explain what their partner said to promote good listening skills.

This activity provides everyone with some talk time when there is a strong desire to share.

Merry-Go-Round

Each student takes a very quick turn sharing with the team a thought or reaction to something posed by the teacher. Responses should be quick one- to five-word phrases in order to keep it going quickly and keep thoughts concise.

This activity allows students to share personal responses in a short time period without recording on paper.

Put Your Two Cents In

Each student has two cowry shells. In groups of four, each student takes a turn by putting one cowry shell in the center of the table and sharing his or her idea. Once everyone has shared once, each student then puts one more cowry shell in the middle and responds to what someone else in the group has shared. For example, "I agree with Juan because . . . " or "I don't agree with Marie because . . . " and so on.

In this activity, students share, question, and support others' opinions.

Circle the Sage

First, the teacher polls the class to see which students have special knowledge to share, such as with homework or understanding a certain topic. Then those students (the sages) stand and spread out in the room. The teacher then has the rest of the class to go to one of the sages, with no two members of the same group going to the same sage. The sages explain what they know while their classmates listen, ask questions, and take notes. All students then return to their original groups. Each student, in turn, explains what they learned. Because most students within the groups have gone to different sages, they compare notes. If there is a disagreement, they stand up as a team. Finally, they state and resolve the disagreements.

Give One, Get One

After thinking or journaling about a topic, students get up and find someone across the room with whom to share their thoughts or answers. Students receive an idea in exchange for giving one.

This activity gives students choice and provides an opportunity for movement.

Three-Step Interview

Each member of a team chooses another member to be a partner. During the first step, students interview their partners by asking interview-type questions. During the second step, partners reverse roles. For the final step, students share their partner's response with the team.

Jigsaw

Teachers create groups of four to five students. Each student is assigned some unique material to learn and then teach to his or her group members. To help in the learning, students from different groups who are focusing on the same material get together to decide what is important and how to teach it. After practice in these "expert" groups, the original groups re-form, and students teach each other. Tests or assessments can follow.

This activity provides interdependency and accountability within a small group.

Team, Pair, Solo

Students do problems first as a team, then with a partner, and finally on their own.

This activity scaffolds learning and motivates students to tackle problems that might initially be beyond their ability.

Roundtable

Teachers organize students into teams of three or four. Students respond to a question or problem by stating their ideas aloud as each member writes them on a single sheet of paper. The paper is then passed around the table until time is called. It is important that students vocalize their ideas as they write so that other team members can reflect on them. Teachers encourage team members not to skip turns. If their thoughts are at a standstill, students can say "pass" once, which keeps the activity moving.

Inner/Outer Circle

Students form two circles with those in the outer circle facing inward and those in the inner circle facing outward. Students in the outer circle begin by asking the student facing them on the inner circle a question. Either students or the teacher can prepare these questions. Once the student in the inner circle has had an opportunity to answer, either the outer or the inner circle rotates, and the process is repeated until a full rotation is made. Then those on the inner circle have the opportunity to ask questions as members of the outer circle respond.

This activity allows for a variety of questions and interactions in a short time span while including movement.

Compiled by Amy Coventry; Sources: Hollie, 2011; Kagan & Kagan, 2009.

Responsive Attention Signals

Effective classroom managers are able to capture the attention of their students at a moment's notice. Attention signals should intrigue students and motivate them to listen attentively as the teacher gives further directions, transitions to a new activity, or winds down the class. We suggest *responsive* attention signals as a way of creating what bell hooks (2005) refers to as a "cultural resonance" with students, giving them something they can relate to while at the same time bringing them to attention. If a teacher already uses traditional attention signals, adding responsive signals to his or her repertoire and using them strategically can make a big difference. Typical traditional signals include the teacher raising his or her hand until the class becomes quiet or flicking the lights on and off. These signals do not necessarily capture some of the students' attention. Responsive signals call for the teacher to do something different to try and capture more students' attention. A responsive attention signal includes some form of *call and response*—the intended interplay or exchange between audience and speaker or student and teacher.

Call-and-response attention signals can be short—for example, one word or a short phrase by both teacher and students. Teachers with students who need more time to focus back can use longer signals, such as chants with multiple phrases. By chanting back, students acknowledge that they know they have a few more seconds before the teacher needs their full attention.

For example, West African Chant is one culturally relevant attention signal technique. Teachers use the West African language Twi to ask students if they are ready to learn by paying attention. They respond "Yes," that they are ready and listening. So the teacher says, "Ah-go" (pay attention), and students reply "Ah-may" (we are listening). We encourage teachers to discover greetings and chants from a variety of languages of their students and incorporate them into attention signals.

Another example is Student Call. In this activity, the teacher signals student attention. He or she calls out the name of the class—for example, "Room 30!"—and students respond with "Woo!

Woo!" or "That's who we are!" Teachers and students decide on the response together to encourage student buy-in. This technique can also include school names and mascots.

Attention signals do not have to include words. With Catch the Beat, the teacher snaps or claps out a rhythm. Students then respond back with the same rhythm. To do this, students must have their hands free to "catch the beat," so they cannot continue writing, cutting, or pasting while responding. The beat changes every time, so students have to listen to hear the rhythm. For example, the teacher claps three times, and then students clap three times. Then the teacher changes the beat to clap, snap, clap, and students respond with clap, snap, clap.

Teachers primarily use attention signals when students are engaged in collaboration or discussion. Most teachers, particularly new teachers, are less likely to use collaborative groups because they feel they will not be able to regain control once students are "let loose" from tight teacher control; however, with a responsive system of attention signals in place, teachers are more likely to use collaborative groups and allow students to work in groups (Hollie, 2011). This speaks directly to the power of a responsive pedagogy and how it can make a difference in instruction, offering the teacher and students options. Teachers who do not have responsive attention signals in their tool kits miss out on using critical techniques, and their students miss out on engaging learning opportunities.

Teachers can have difficulty with attention signals—specifically with knowing when to use them and how often to use them. Attention signals "get students back" during and after an activity, but they may not necessarily get students quiet—a fundamental difference. A lack of understanding of this difference can lead to overuse of a particular attention signal. Wolfe (2001) says that using attention signals proves useful over time because of habituation, but doing the same type of attention signal can be ineffective. Flicking the light switch to get students' attention may work well the first few times, but with extended use, students often are less likely to respond as quickly. While teachers must commit to the use of attention signals, they must also commit to using a variety of signals.

Table 8.2 provides an additional sampling of effective and responsive attention signals used by educators who have gone through our trainings.

Table 8.2: Examples of Effective Attention Signals for Responsive Classroom Management

Voice Check
Voice Check is used to change the volume of student voices in the classroom. The teacher says, "Voice check" in the tone and level of volume in which he or she wants the students to respond. The students then respond, "One, two . . . one, two!"
For example, a teacher whispers, "Voice check," and students whisper "One, two . . . one, two!" when students are working in a lab and expected to talk softly.

Holla Back
The teacher calls out a phrase from a popular song, and the students respond with the second word of the song. For example, a teacher says, "Holla!" and students respond with "Back!" (The teacher is free to use any two words he or she chooses.)

When I Move, You Move
Teachers can use this technique during transition times when students are getting materials out or going to other places in the classroom. The teacher calls out or raps, "When I move, you move!" and the students call back, "Just like that!"

When I Say . . .
In this technique, the teacher gives directions during the call and response. For example, the teacher says, "When I say peace, you say quiet." Then the teacher says, "Peace," and the students respond with, "Quiet." The teacher can change the words in this chant to fit the situation.

Chant
These are longer signals that give students more time to bring their attention back to the teacher. For example, the teacher chants, "One, two," and students reply, "Eyes on you." The teacher says "Three, four," and students reply, "I talk no more." The teacher says, "Five, six," and the students reply, "We play no tricks." The teacher says, "Seven, eight," and the students say, "Sit up straight." Finally, the teacher says, "Nine, ten," and students say, "We're ready to begin!"

Give Me Five
This signal technique asks students to have their hands free while responding to the teacher. The teacher raises his or her hand, and then students also raise their hand back to give the teacher a high five in the air. The teacher can then ask students to give a high five to one another.
Give Yourself Some Love
Teachers use this technique to acknowledge students for their successes as a whole group. The teacher tells the students, "Hands up! Hands down! Hands out! Hands in! Now give yourself some love." The students wrap their arms around themselves, creating a hug.
Head, Shoulders, Knees, and Toes
When students are restless, the teacher tells them to touch body parts at varying speeds. For example, the teacher says in a singsong voice, "Hands on your head. Hands on your knees. Hands on your elbows." Then he or she speeds up the pace and says, "On your cheeks. On your nose. On your tummy." And then the teacher either slows the pace down or goes even faster, saying, "Hands on your chin. Hands on your forehead. Hands on your shoulders. On your mouth. On your eyes, and on your toes."
Brain Break
When students are restless, moving around, or getting talkative, the teacher calls out, "Brain break!" Then the teacher leads the class in various activities, such as yoga stretches or relaxation breathing.

Compiled by Kiechelle Russell.

Responsive Movement Activities

Adding movement activities to instruction provides extra sensory input to the brain and enhances learning (Wolfe, 2001). Jensen (2003) reports that brain researchers have verified that sensory motor integration is fundamental to school readiness. Other research has shown that there may be a link between violent tendencies in school and outside of school and a lack of movement (Kotulak, 1996).

Students need to move while learning. Therefore, movement should be part of the responsive pedagogy. Teachers should infuse movement into the activities and techniques they use in their classrooms. By having students move frequently and with purpose, teachers can actually decrease classroom-management issues, such as off-task behavior, excessive talking, and boredom. Movement increases student engagement overall, and when students are engaged they are less likely to misbehave or be off task. Many of the techniques we've suggested for responsive classroom management and responsive attention signals and in tables 8.1 and 8.2 (pages 103–105 and 108–109) involve movement and can be easily infused into everyday teaching, such as Circle the Sage; Inner/Outer Circle; Head, Shoulders, Knees, and Toes; and Brain Break.

In another activity, Musical Shares, the teacher plays upbeat music for students, who then dance around the room. At some point, the music stops and students have to stop dancing and solve a problem or share their answers with one another to a question the teacher has posed. After a few moments, the music starts again, and the students resume dancing around the room. The music stops again, and the process repeats for as long as the teacher desires. This activity keeps students engaged in the learning while they move, and it also presents an opportunity for teachers to include culturally relevant music that connects to students' home and community life.

Building Responsive Classroom Management

In this chapter, we have examined what makes practices in classroom management responsive. The responsive pedagogy of an effectively managed system is collaborative, focuses on techniques for responding and discussing, and effectively uses attention signals and movement activities. Using these techniques frequently and on an ongoing basis increases student engagement and decreases classroom-management issues.

In the next chapter, we examine the second area of instruction—responsive academic vocabulary—and explore specific activities to use in vocabulary instruction. Before you move on to the next chapter, reflect on the questions that follow.

CHAPTER 8
Reflections

1 In general, what philosophy for classroom management is in place at your school site? What is your individual philosophy?

2 Does your school or district have a schoolwide classroom management system or program in place? How would you describe its quality?

3 Of the three focus areas of responsive classroom management, which is an area of strength for you (or your staff), and which is an area of weakness?

4 Which responsive attention signals could you use immediately or juxtapose with a traditional attention signal? What movement activities could you use?

Nine

Responsive Academic Vocabulary

Think back to your school experience. How did you learn vocabulary in elementary and middle school? Like most people, your vocabulary development probably involved (1) a list of twenty words connected to an upcoming text in a certain content area, (2) looking up those words in a glossary or dictionary, (3) attempting to use those words in a sentence or a story, and (4) a quiz on Friday. On the surface, this traditional approach to learning vocabulary makes sense. Students are exposed to words weekly, they practice those words and teachers reinforce them through a variety of formats, and students take a weekly assessment to monitor and support their learning.

We know more about vocabulary instruction today than we did back then; we can easily argue the ineffectiveness of pieces of the traditional approach (Graves, 2006). It is like asking someone to bring an eight-track cassette to a party that is playing MP3 files only. The MP3 files of today's vocabulary instruction focus students on vocabulary acquisition in a robust, authentic manner.

Four Key Premises

Although the time of the traditional approach to teaching vocabulary has long passed, we can't dismiss all of the knowledge from that era. A survey of the literature clearly indicates that the following principles of vocabulary instruction should be included in any program or approach (Beck, McKeown, & Kucan, 2002; Stahl, 1999):

- Provide definitional and contextual information about a word's meaning.

- Actively involve students in word learning through talking about, comparing, analyzing, and using the target words.

- Provide students with multiple exposures to meaningful information about each word.

- Teach word analysis.

When working with students, especially underserved students, teachers must consider these time-proven concepts. Activating prior knowledge, making schematic connections, and building on the words that students already know are the core of any basic vocabulary instruction. In addition, teachers who have a responsive pedagogy in academic vocabulary acknowledge four key philosophical premises (Hollie, 2011).

Premise One

Students have a comprehensive conceptual knowledge base that is rooted in their culture, community, and life experiences. They develop thoughts and opinions about the world around them, and they use their own labels to describe concepts they encounter. We call these the words students "own," and they often differ from the academic words students are expected to know and learn in school. Responsive vocabulary instruction builds and expands on these words as a bridge to academic vocabulary. Traditional vocabulary instruction does not generally expand on students' own words in this way. Responsive vocabulary instruction seeks to develop students' concepts of words, not simply ask them to memorize meaning. When teachers just teach words without making schematic connections to concepts, they are decreasing the opportunities for students to own academic vocabulary.

Premise Two

A common question asked in vocabulary instruction is, What does a proficient reader do when coming across a word that he or she does not know? (Krashen, 2004). In traditional instruction, struggling readers are often told to go to the dictionary when they come across a word they do not know. However, proficient readers use *acquisition strategies* to figure out what the word means, not the dictionary (Stahl, 1999). Teachers of underserved students must focus on recommended key vocabulary strategies for word acquisition, not simple word memorization. Acquisition strategies include wide and abundant reading, contextualization and conceptualization of words, knowledge of word parts, and use of synonyms (Stahl, 1999). Ample practice with these strategies becomes integral to expanding students' academic vocabularies.

Premise Three

How we think about word usage can be related to our linguistic background or home language. For some English learners and nonstandard language speakers, such as speakers of Black English and Chicano English, synonymous usage of words is not commonplace. Rather, one word or phrase can have multiple meanings. For example, in African American Vernacular English (AAVE), terms like *bad* and *get* remain constant in usage regardless of the ever-changing meanings. There are essentially three uses of *bad* in AAVE: the bad *bad*, meaning not good; the good or awesome *bad*; and the now common phrase, "My bad," said to offer contrition. *Get* has numerous meanings as well: Get down. Get out of here. Get real. Get me a soda. Getting on my nerves. Get it straight. Get your groove on. Get with it. In contrast, Standard English speakers might vary the word or phrase with the meaning, therefore employing synonymous usage, such as replacing *get* with *bring* in the phrase "Bring me a soda." Teachers skilled in expanding academic vocabulary, especially in English learners and nonstandard language speakers, recognize this dynamic and make instructional modifications.

Premise Four

Many educators see slang as nonstandard language; they do not consider it a part of real vocabulary. However, in responsive vocabulary instruction, teachers recognize that slang (even profanity and racially charged terms) can become sources of academic expansion. Generally speaking, teenagers and young adults are the primary users of slang; it is a part of youth culture. Educators must respond to it in validating and affirming ways so that they can bridge students' conceptual vocabularies to academic vocabulary. Teachers can also influence students' word choices and help them develop situational appropriateness as they navigate in academic settings and negotiate mainstream culture. In order to do this, educators must view slang as a positive to expand upon, not as a negative to restrict.

Steps for Responsive Vocabulary Instruction

The four premises provide a theoretical underpinning teachers can build on within the area of vocabulary instruction to make their teaching more responsive. For example, at CLAS and in his work with teachers and students across the United States, author Sharroky Hollie (2011) uses a process that reflects the four premises and creates a responsive approach to vocabulary instruction. His process includes:

1. Leveling words

2. Using vocabulary-acquisition strategies: context clues, word parts, and synonym and antonym development for deeper understanding of content-specific words

3. Using common vocabulary strategies for meaning development and richer representation

Step One: Leveling Words

In *Bringing Words to Life* (2002), Beck et al. assert that the teacher has the creative, but informed, license to determine what words students should acquire for a given lesson or text. Teachers know their students better than the authors of an anthology, so responsive teachers customize their selection of words to fit students' specific needs. Beck et al. explain that words can be divided into three tiers or levels: words that students already know or common everyday words (level 1), words that students should know as mature language users (level 2), and words that students should be familiar with but will rarely encounter in print or in speech (level 3).

The level 2 words are the ones that should be the focus for vocabulary acquisition in general and, in particular, for English learners and nonstandard language users. They include words that have importance, utility, and instructional potential, and they can be taught in a variety of ways so that students can build rich representations and connect these words to other words and concepts, including those they already own.

Most basal anthologies provide a list of words that students should know for each unit, chapter, or story. These are usually words that students will not know. Leveling words involves dividing the list into the three levels. Level 2 should contain five to seven words that will become the focus of vocabulary acquisition and instruction. Teachers strategically select these words because they will give the students the most "mileage" in usage as readers, writers, and speakers. Teachers should cover these words before and during instruction so students will be able to navigate the text successfully.

Step Two: Using Vocabulary-Acquisition Strategies

In this step of teaching vocabulary, responsive teachers use key strategies: context clues and synonym development (Graves, 2006) and antonym development. With context clues, the teacher creates sentences or a brief paragraph in which level 2 words are embedded in the text. Students then guess at the meanings using the context clues. Since the teacher is more interested in the conceptual meanings than the technical meanings, students will initially provide definitions of what they think a word means from their own vocabularies. Teachers must keep in mind that the meanings students develop for words will not be exact at this point. It is important to listen for the conceptual understanding of the word because if students have a conceptual understanding, they will be able to expand their vocabularies.

For example, the teacher presents students with a list of level 2 focus words—*tedious*, *detest*, and *parch*—and then engages students in an exercise to practice the strategy of using context clues. Figure 9.1 illustrates this activity.

Target Word in Context	This is what I THINK the word means.	What were the clues in the sentence that helped me guess?	This is MY WORD for the target word.
The assignment was so tedious that he started to fall asleep.	Boring	Started to fall asleep	Boring
I detest bell peppers because they make me sick.	Hate	Make me sick	Hate
Coming from a long, grueling basketball practice, my throat was parched.	Very thirsty	Long, grueling	Thirsty

Figure 9.1: Context clue exercise.

Another responsive activity for vocabulary acquisition involves using two instructional tools that validate and affirm vocabulary learning for students (Hollie, 2011). The first tool is the Personal Thesaurus (PT). The PT is a graphic organizer in booklet form that helps students visualize the process of expanding from home vocabulary, from a word with which they are already comfortable, to a word that is more appropriate for academic speaking and writing. The PT is best used with level 2 words because students are most likely to have conceptual understanding of these words. The Personal Dictionary (PD), based on the Frayer Model (Frayer, Frederick, & Klausmeier, 1969) or four square, is another graphic organizer tool. The PD is used with level 3 words only because they tend to be content specific and low frequency in text. The PD helps students learn the word along with the concept. Both tools give students ownership of the words they are learning, and hence they are responsive.

How to Use the Personal Thesaurus

Students take the words from the context clue activity to create their Personal Thesaurus. From the example in figure 9.1, students would take their words from column four—*boring, hate,* and *thirsty*—and add them to the boxes at the top of the PT (see figure 9.2 on page 120). The target words—*tedious, detest,* and *parched*—go on the first lines directly below the boxes. Then, the teacher asks students to brainstorm additional words for the target concepts that they already have in their own vocabulary. These words, which will eventually become synonyms for the target vocabulary word, indicate their understanding of the concept of the target word, not the exact meaning. In the example, these words are *dull, loathe,* and *dehydrated*. Students write them on the other lines below their word and the target word. Students continue to add to their booklet, creating their own personal thesaurus for use during their writing and speaking in academic situations. Making connections between students' own words and the academic words they are expected to learn is what makes the activity responsive.

This activity can also be used to bridge students' use of slang to the academic vocabulary. We acknowledge that slang is most often seen as linguistically inappropriate in the context of school; however, youth do use this vocabulary, and educators can use it as an opportunity to teach academic vocabulary. We have found this responsive strategy to be successful with underserved students in particular. For these students, slang has a value steeped in descriptive, colorful use of words.

To make the bridge between slang and academic language, we recommend a process called "academization." In this activity, students provide a slang word and its meaning and the teacher provides the academic term, therefore academizing the students' slang words (Hollie, 2011). For example, a current popular slang term is *swag*. In slang terms, one definition of *swag* is really cool, funky, and positive. Students will sometimes refer to one another as being *swag*. Upon hearing the use of the term, the teacher inquires as to its meaning. The teacher validates and affirms the students when asking them to share the definition of a word they own. Then the teacher provides an academic word to replace the slang in school or academic language. A possible academic translation for the term *swag* is *confident*. Once the students and teacher agree on the academic term, students enter both words in their PT and continue the process by brainstorming synonyms.

Personal Thesaurus (PT) Chart

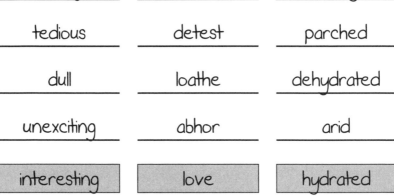

Figure 9.2: Sample Personal Thesaurus page.

How to Use the Personal Dictionary

For content areas such as math, science, social studies, and language arts, vocabulary words have more specific meanings that students typically do not have background knowledge of or previous concepts for. These are the level 3 words. Thus, teachers must use a different strategy for instruction in these content areas because students will have difficulty generating synonyms. We suggest a tool called the Personal Dictionary (PD). Figure 9.3 shows an example of a PD for a language arts class. In the figure, the academic term in the content area is *personification*. Students first apply a technical definition and then develop an illustration and a personal connection. The illustration and connection are what help students associate with the content and relate to it, allowing for recall (Frayer et al., 1969). Students build their own dictionary of content-specific words by creating a collection of 5 × 7 index cards or PowerPoint slides. Figures 9.4 and 9.5 (page 122) show two more examples of PDs.

Academic Term	Personal Illustration
Personification	
Technical Definition	**Personal Connections**
A representation, usually of an inanimate object made animate	The clock spoke to me directly, "You are late for the show."

Figure 9.3: Language arts example of a Personal Dictionary for *personification*.

Academic Term	Personal Illustration
Adjacent	1 2 3 4 5 6
Personal Connection	**Personal Definition**
I am adjacent to my friend when I sit next to her in class.	It is a word that means being next to something or someone.

Figure 9.4: Math example of a Personal Dictionary for *adjacent*.

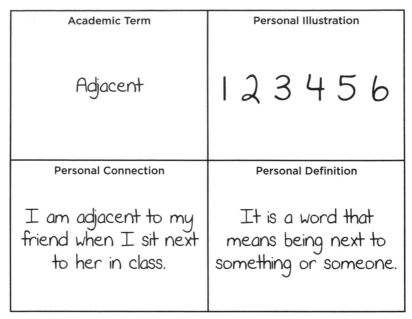

Academic Term	Personal Illustration
Atmosphere	
Personal Connection	**Personal Definition**
I see the atmosphere when I look up at the sky.	It is a word that means the part of the sky that starts from the ground and goes far above the earth.

Figure 9.5: Science example of a Personal Dictionary for *atmosphere*.

Step Three: Using Common Vocabulary Strategies for Meaning Development and Richer Representation

Once the teacher and students work to transform words students own into an academic vocabulary, responsive teachers give students multiple opportunities to engage and interact with the new words and practice the new vocabulary acquisition strategies they are learning. Teachers should keep in mind that the goal of reinforcement and practice activities is to provide students with as many exposures to the word as possible. The end result for level 2 words in particular is ownership, when students' word knowledge demonstrates precision or availability so that they can both understand a word and apply it in a variety of contexts.

Each reinforcement and review activity gives the teacher an opportunity to informally assess students and engage in discussions that help them explore facets of word meaning and consider relationships among words. This builds student confidence, which is particularly important for underserved students who struggle and moves students toward assessment readiness. Examples of reinforcement activities include CLOZE activities, vocabulary charades, and password, to name a few. The reader is strongly encouraged to see Carleton and Marzano's (2010) book *Vocabulary Games* for a plethora of activities, in addition to Janet Allen's (1999) *Words, Words, Words*.

Building Responsive Academic Vocabulary

The quality of a student's academic vocabulary is directly related to his or her success in reading, writing, and speaking. Responsive teachers understand the four premises and use them as a basis for instruction by infusing responsive strategies and activities into their traditional instructional activities, such as leveling words, using vocabulary acquisition strategies that encourage student movement from language they own to academic language, and developing richer representation with reinforcement.

In the next chapter, we examine the third area—responsive academic literacy—in greater depth and explore specific activities to use in instruction. Before you move on to the next chapter, reflect on the questions that follow.

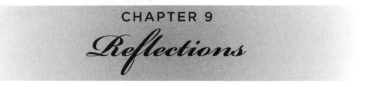

CHAPTER 9
Reflections

1   Typically, how do you select words for your vocabulary teaching?

2   What regular vocabulary activities do you currently employ to reinforce learning? How do responsive techniques to vocabulary instruction differ from your approaches?

3   To what extent will you or others in your school buy in to building on the words students bring to school? What about slang?

4   Do you provide students with many opportunities to engage and interact with new vocabulary once they have transformed the words they own into academic vocabulary? How could you do more of this reinforcement?

Ten

Responsive Academic Literacy

As we've discussed in earlier chapters, strong literacy skills—reading, writing, listening, and speaking—support student success in almost all other academic subjects. Research has found that not only are many underserved students doing poorly in reading (National Association for the Advancement of Colored People, 2011), but most of those who struggle are performing just as poorly in math and other subject areas (Krashen, 2004). Beyond schooling, literacy skills have a direct impact on students' success in life. According to research ("Illiteracy: The downfall," 2011), adults with the lowest levels of literacy are almost ten times as likely to live below the poverty line and three times as likely to receive food stamps as other adults. Unfortunately, many teachers have become accustomed to the discouraging statistics related to reading. Since increased literacy skills are a key to students' overall academic success, teachers must place a particular focus on building academic literacy skills for all students, especially those who struggle.

The strategic building of students' literacy skills depends on teachers' responsive use of text, including all types of print, fiction and nonfiction, in a variety of forms, such as newspapers, magazines, journals, reports, and web media. To be responsive in academic literacy, we suggest teachers focus on three strategies to effectively reach students:

1. Engaging students with culturally responsive texts

2. Using read-alouds in the oral tradition of cultural storytelling

3. Using responsive research-based literacy techniques

Engaging Students With Culturally Responsive Texts

The chance of finding a variety of authentic pieces of culturally responsive text in mandated curricula, commercial programs, or the standard content of textbooks is slim. In general, publishers have done a better job in recent years of representing more cultures in an accessible manner in their books, but these attempts are still largely tokenistic and include the most-known authors of the past (Harris, 1999). For example, one of the authors asked a publisher to send him a selection of culturally responsive literature from an anthology so he could prepare for a presentation at a reading conference. It was not surprising that the publisher sent classic works by the African American authors Langston Hughes and Gwendolyn Brooks—*A Dream Deferred* and *We Be Cool*. True, these are certainly culturally responsive texts, but they are overused and have lost their appeal over time, especially as students are exposed to them over multiple years.

Educators cannot expect textbooks mandated by the state to be culturally responsive. Teachers must plan to supplement the state-mandated curriculum with texts that are culturally engaging to students. Underserved students need a wide array of culturally relevant choices. Culturally responsive texts allow students to relate their life experiences to academics, and they are then able to make better connections to mainstream (traditional) texts. Diverse texts not only include issues of race, but appeal to issues of gender, age, and socioeconomics as well.

We offer the following suggestions for selecting culturally responsive texts:

- Choose well-known authors, illustrators, publishers, and book sellers who have already developed solid reputations. Many times, cultures are presented in a generalized, stereotyped way within texts. Choosing professionals with proven track records often keeps the selection process from being a guessing game. They can often be trusted to be culturally authentic and avoid the limitations of generalizations and stereotypes.

- Critically analyze how the characters are portrayed in the story, how the facts are presented, and in what context. The text should not simply be a compilation of generalizations and stereotypes about a certain group. This is critical because the goal of choosing culturally responsive material is for students to be able to relate to it.

- Evaluate factual information for accuracy, and, when applicable, analyze the author's use of nonstandard language for authenticity.

- Carefully examine illustrations for appeal, ethnic sensitivity, and authenticity (LeMoine, 1998).

The overall goal in the selection process is to find culturally responsive texts of all types that match mainstream titles in theme or topic and that focus on the same standards. We prescribe that for every mainstream title, state standard, or topic covered in a class, there should be at least one reading or interaction with a piece of text that is culturally responsive for all students. It is incumbent on the teacher to seek stories, poems, essays, articles, songs, or any text that students can relate to.

For example, at CLAS, middle school students read two texts correlated to a theme. For the theme of "youth rebellion," they might read *The Outsiders,* a mainstream title, and *A Hero Ain't Nothing But a Sandwich*, a responsive text. Both of these books deal with coming-of-age issues, but in two completely different ways. *The Outsiders* follows two rival groups, the Greasers and the Socs, in a small Midwestern town who are divided by their socioeconomic status. *A Hero Ain't Nothing But a Sandwich* is set in Harlem and follows a young African American boy as he struggles with heroin addiction. Underserved students most benefit from responsive text selections because they can relate to the characters or the setting, so they become more fully engaged in the text. Teachers can then use this engagement as a bridge to the mainstream texts. In schools with a variety of cultures represented, teachers should reflect this variety in their choices of responsive texts. Table 10.1 provides some additional suggestions. (See www.culturallyresponsive.org for a full list of suggested culturally responsive titles.)

Table 10.1: Examples of culturally responsive texts.

Grades K–2	
Be Boy Buzz	My Nana and Me
Earth Mother	The Hat That Wore Clara B.
Henry's Freedom Box	This Jazz Man
In the Hollow of Your Hand	What's Cooking, Jamela?
Langston's Train Ride	
Grades 3–5	
As Good as Anybody Else	Sienna's Scrapbook
Brothers in Hope	Story Painter
Growing Up: It's a Girl Thing	Working Cotton
Here in Harlem	A Young Dancer
Michael's Golden Rules	
Grades 6–12	
Afrikan Alphabets	Harlem Summer
Burro Genius	How the Garcia Girls Lost Their Accents
Change Has Come	On My Own Journey Now
Enrique's Journey	Wake Up Our Souls
Graffiti Girl	

Using Read-Alouds in the Oral Tradition of Storytelling

Inherent to responsive pedagogy in literacy is engaging students who might be otherwise disengaged, unmotivated, and/or turned off to the idea of reading as a source of pleasure, entertainment, and knowledge. Many cultures, such as the African American, Latino, and Polynesian cultures, have a rich history of storytelling, and reading aloud in school complements this history. It is a powerful way to connect to students culturally and build literacy skills. In addition, when students listen to other readers, it stimulates growth and understanding of vocabulary and language patterns (Trelease, 2001). There are many benefits of reading aloud, especially for students who do not speak Standard English as their first language. Reading aloud can help these students become more fluent and competent readers. However, it is important not to put English learners or nonproficient readers on the spot. These students need plenty of time to experience receptive language (listening) while they are becoming more confident with expressive language (speaking and reading aloud).

Read-aloud activities can be as simple as a Teacher Read in which the teacher reads the text aloud, modeling the prosodic features of the language, and students listen and follow along in their books. This activity is beneficial because students hear a proficient reader reading the text and it has a low affective filter (student anxiety is low).

Read-aloud activities can also be much more complex, such as with Fade In and Fade Out. In this activity, the teacher uses nonverbal cues to indicate which student will read. He or she walks around the room and touches the shoulder of a student. This student starts to read in a whisper and then raises the volume to a normal reading voice. As the first student reads, the teacher touches another student's shoulder. That student then begins reading in a whisper, and the student who was reading fades out, going from a normal volume to a whisper. When in sync, this activity models fluency in a strong way because students must pay careful attention to the intonation, pace, and flow of the reading.

These are just two examples of read-aloud activities that could be part of a responsive pedagogy in academic literacy. The staff at CLAS uses a variety of read-aloud activities to model fluent reading, guide oral reading, and give students the opportunity to practice (Hollie, 2011).

Train Reading

In this technique, the teacher chooses three to five students ahead of time and tells them they will read when directed. The teacher is the engine—he or she starts as the first reader. The teacher then chooses proficient readers to continue the reading—the cars and caboose in the reading train. The benefits are that proficient readers can model fluency and prosodic features for struggling students.

Popcorn Reading

This activity is very engaging for students as they have the power to choose who reads aloud. A student begins to read the text and says, "Popcorn [student's name]," choosing another student to pick up where he or she left off in the text, or the teacher can popcorn and choose proficient readers. Students feel empowered in selecting who reads next, they are highly engaged, and the activity is student centered; however, if less-proficient readers are chosen, they may stall the reading experience. Although students choose who reads, the teacher might provide some guidance and assist students who struggle.

Jump-In Reading

With this technique, students have the autonomy to choose when they would like to participate and read aloud by "jumping in." A student can jump in whenever he or she chooses, as long as it is at a period stop. Students must read at least three sentences, and they can read for as long as they want or until someone jumps in. If two or more students jump in at the same time, they must decide who will read by one deferring to the other. The reader can also choose to stop reading, which might produce a few moments of silence. This is perfectly acceptable. Moments of silence allow students to think and reflect about what was just read. Eventually, another student will jump in. This activity is highly engaging for students, it has a low affective filter, and it is student centered.

Echo Reading

In this activity, the teacher reads one sentence, paragraph, or section and then stops. Students echo the teacher by reading the same sentence in the same way. The pros are that it's great for modeling prosody and a sense of cooperation, and it has a low affective filter; however, students might choose not to participate.

Buddy Reading

In this activity, teachers assign groups of student buddies with one proficient reader reading to his or her nonproficient partner. This can be done with students in the same grade level or class or with an upper-grade student and a lower-grade student. Students can keep the same buddy throughout the school year or semester. The benefits are that students are motivated to work with peers, they are engaged, there is a low affective filter, and the activity is student centered.

Choral Reading

Just as a choir sings in unison, in this activity, the teacher leads his or her students to read together in one voice. The teacher points out where to start in the passage and cues students to read. All students are expected to read together. The benefit of this activity is that it has a low affective filter, but some students may lack engagement.

Radio Reading

With this activity, teachers choose proficient readers to read a text in different voices. Students are asked to relay emotion with their voice, such a happy, sad, sleepy, and so on. They can also choose a voice type, such as an old woman, a child, a baby, and so on. Teachers choose readers before the activity so the students can practice their voice of choice. The benefit is that students are highly engaged in the activity; however, the activity is limited to proficient readers, and it's possible for listeners to lose track of the storyline and focus on the reader instead.

Using Responsive Literacy Techniques Effectively

Responsive literacy techniques and activities offer a source of motivation and interest to students, thus increasing engagement, particularly for underserved students. These techniques and activities differ from traditional instruction because they maximize student interest and involvement with either direct instruction, inquiry, or an interactive format (Echevarria & Graves, 2011). After reviewing a comprehensive set of literacy research (Norton & Land, 2007), we have identified a set of effective literacy activities that are suited for a responsive pedagogy. These are suggestions based on our experience working with hundreds of teachers across the United States and at CLAS. They are a part of a responsive pedagogy, and we offer them not as a prescription, but as a description of what responsive instruction looks like in the area of academic literacy.

Language Experience Approach for Sight Word Development

In this activity (Krashen, 2004), students dictate their own story based on the sight word list, individually or in groups, as the teacher records it. This strategy increases the likelihood that students, particularly struggling readers, will be able to read and comprehend the text since the words are their own and correspond with students' cultural and linguistic experiences.

After the dictation is complete, the teacher reads the story aloud, pointing to each word as students follow along. This helps build a sight word vocabulary for words that students already know as part of a speaking vocabulary but have not yet learned in written form. As the teacher reads the story, students have the opportunity to make changes. Once the story is final, the teacher and students read it together, with the teacher again pointing to each word.

Students then try reading the story alone. If there are any words that they cannot pronounce, the teacher makes note of these for later practice and review. These words might go into a personal word bank or on a word wall where they serve as individual dictionaries for future reference for reading or for writing stories.

When the teacher feels confident that students have mastered the words as sight words, students can rewrite the story and illustrate it as an additional activity, either in groups or individually.

We recommend this activity for word recognition and vocabulary development.

Phonograms: Hink Pinks, Hinky Pinkies, Hinkety Pinketies

In this activity (Norton & Land, 2007), the teacher introduces a book that incorporates multiple rhyming words by doing a "walk of pictures" (a gallery). The teacher encourages students to listen to the story and explains that they are going to be listening for words that sound alike at the end, such as *frog* and *log*. The teacher then reads the story while the class listens.

During reading, the teacher briefly pauses several times to prompt students to orally name a word that rhymes with a word from the story. After reading, the teacher explains that she is going to give some clues and the class will have to think of rhyming words to guess the riddle. At least one of the words the students will be guessing should come from the story. For example, if the book includes a fish, one clue and answer could be "a dream or request made by a water animal from our story" (fish ➜ wish).

For those learners having difficulty guessing the answers to the riddles, the teacher can provide one of the words in the *hink pink* (the rhyming words that answer the clue), and the students try and guess the second rhyming word. [In this activity, pairs of words that are one-syllable answers to riddles are called *hink pinks*, while answers of two syllables are called *hinky pinkies*, and three-syllable answers are called *hinkety pinketies*. For example: frog-log (hink pink), gory-story (hinky pinkie), and robbery-snobbery (hinkety pinkety).]

The teacher could also begin by giving one word in the *hink pink* to provide scaffolding. Gradually, she would give the clues in written format and let the class guess both rhyming words. Eventually, students can create their own riddles with rhyming words as answers.

This activity is recommended for word recognition and vocabulary building.

Thinking Maps

Thinking Maps™, developed by David Hyerle, are visual organizers used consistently to frame seven particular types of thinking.

These tools are different from graphic organizers because they should be used exclusively, for the most part, to organize the types of thinking most often required in an educational setting: defining in context, comparing and contrasting, categorizing and classifying, analogies, whole to part, describing, cause and effect/problem and solution, and sequencing. They are also different from graphic organizers because they are flexible. They are adjustable to an activity, and students are able to draw them independently.

This activity can be used before, during, and after reading. Thinking Maps include circle maps, tree maps, bubble maps, double bubble maps, flow maps, multi-flow maps, brace maps, and bridge maps.

Reader's Theater

This activity involves the performance, by an individual or a group, of a literary work in which the text is read expressively, but not fully staged and acted out. It provides fluency practice and can be used during or after reading.

SQ3R

The SQ3R strategy is a widely recognized study system that is easily adapted to reading assignments. This method provides concrete steps for interacting with information that results in high levels of comprehension. SQ3R stands for the following five steps:

1. Survey—The reader previews the material to develop a general outline for organizing information.

2. Question—The reader raises questions with the expectation of finding answers in the material.

3. Read—The reader attempts to answer the questions he or she formulated in the previous step.

4. Recite—The reader deliberately attempts to answer out loud or in writing the questions he or she formulated in the second step.

5. Review—The reader reviews the material by rereading portions of the assignment in order to verify the answers he or she gave during the previous step.

We recommend using this activity before, during, and after reading expository text.

Reciprocal Teaching

Reciprocal teaching, as described by Palincsar (1986), is an instructional activity that takes place in the form of a dialogue between teachers and students (and eventually among students) regarding segments of text. The dialogue is structured by the use of four strategies: summarizing, question generating, clarifying, and predicting. The teacher and students take turns assuming the role of teacher in leading the dialogue. Reciprocal teaching facilitates a group effort between teacher and students, as well as among students, to bring meaning to the text. The strategies have the following purposes.

Summarizing provides students with the opportunity to identify and integrate the most important information in the text. Students can summarize sentences, paragraphs, and entire texts. When they first begin the reciprocal teaching activity, their efforts are generally focused at the sentence and paragraph levels. As they become more proficient, they are able to summarize at the paragraph and passage levels.

Question generating reinforces the summarizing strategy and moves the learner one more step toward comprehension. When students generate questions, they first identify the kind of information that is significant enough to provide the substance for a question. They then pose this information in question form and self-test it. This is a flexible strategy because students can generate questions at many levels. For example, sometimes students are called upon to master supporting detail information, while other times they are required to infer or apply new information from text.

Clarifying is particularly important when working with students who have a history of comprehension difficulty. These struggling students may believe that the purpose of reading is saying the words correctly; they may not be particularly uncomfortable that the words, and in fact the passage, are not making sense. When the teacher asks these students to clarify, it calls their attention to the fact that there are many reasons why text is difficult to understand (such as new vocabulary, unclear reference words, and unfamiliar and perhaps difficult concepts). Students are taught to be alert to such difficulties and to take the necessary measures to restore meaning (such as rereading or asking for help).

Predicting is when students hypothesize what the author will discuss next in the text. To do this successfully, students must activate the relevant background knowledge that they already possess regarding a topic. The students have a purpose for reading: to confirm or disprove their hypotheses. Furthermore, students have the opportunity to link the new knowledge they will encounter in the text with the knowledge they already possess. The predicting strategy also facilitates use of text structure as students learn that headings, subheadings, and questions embedded in the text are useful means of anticipating what might occur next.

We recommend using this activity before, during, and after reading.

Anticipation/Reaction Guide

An anticipation/reaction guide increases reading comprehension by stimulating prior knowledge and experiences before reading, and then reinforcing key concepts after reading. It gives students a series of leading questions (written by the teacher) that they must answer in writing before reading. Students then share their answers in a class discussion designed specifically to activate or reactivate prior knowledge. This review of prior knowledge helps students connect with the topic. Students then read the text passage and evaluate their written answers (prior knowledge). Students should note when their answers agree or disagree with the text's content. Finally, students engage in a summarizing discussion, expressing how the reading reinforced or challenged their prior knowledge.

We recommend using this activity before and after reading.

Hot Seat

In this activity, students read part or all of a selected piece of literature. The teacher divides the class into groups of three to five students. Each student selects a character whose persona he or she will adopt and prepares for an interrogation from the rest of the class. All students (working independently or in groups) should prepare questions for each character. Questions may focus on recalling the story or dealing with a character's emotions. Hot Seat formats vary with the group of students. Teachers may ask a panel of characters to assume the "hot seat" or limit it to individuals. Teachers might also use puppets, character masks, or murals for this activity. This activity can be used after reading.

Can You Feel Me?

This strategy (Hollie, 2011) gives validity to students' personal reactions to selected pieces of writing; allows students to express their reactions in a nonjudgmental setting, draws images together from all points of a poem, a story, or prose; and allows students to reflect and select unforgettable mental pictures.

In this activity, students read a selection silently and independently. They then select and highlight words, phrases, or sentences that they find particularly meaningful or that create vivid mental images for them. Teachers then invite students to participate in a voluntary, random sharing of their selected images. Students read aloud "as the spirit moves them." While one person reads, other students should listen. Teachers should be active participants in this activity and allow for periods of silence. This activity can be used after reading.

Building Responsive Academic Literacy

In this chapter, we learned that to be skilled with the use of text, teachers must accomplish three tasks: consistently and appropriately select culturally responsive texts that supplement the core instructional program; effectively use read-alouds, which simulate the cultural norm of storytelling for many students; and use responsive literacy strategies. Above all, teachers must remember that strong literacy skills influence student success overall and that choosing effective techniques and activities will help them engage students.

In the next chapter, we examine the fourth and final area—a responsive learning environment—in greater depth. Before you move on to the next chapter, reflect on the questions that follow.

CHAPTER 10
Reflections

1 What is the current literacy achievement data in your school or district? What student populations are having success? What populations are failing?

2 To what degree are the texts in your school responsive to the cultural backgrounds of the student population?

3 To what extent do all teachers, across all content areas, use read-alouds to engage students and connect to their cultural background of storytelling?

4 To what extent do all teachers, across all content areas, use common and effective reading strategies?

Eleven

Responsive Learning Environment

Understanding the relationship between environment and behavior enables teachers to organize and equip their classrooms so that students are more likely to achieve optimal learning. In Charlotte Danielson's (2007) framework for teaching, she identifies the organization of physical space as a key component to an effective learning environment. A strategically arranged environment creates the spatial context in which movement and learning activities take place. Barbara Shade and her colleagues note that an inviting learning environment is a pleasant physical and psychological atmosphere that welcomes students (Shade, Kelly, & Oberg, 1997). All learners, especially underserved learners, thrive in environments that are intentionally stimulating.

Responsive learning environments are also culturally relevant to students, reflecting students' unique home and community backgrounds. Moos (1979) said that for children of color and families of immigration, their initial assessment of their acceptance into the school environment depends on whether or not they perceive pictures, symbols, and other visual representations that remind them of their homes, communities, and values. This concept is the basis of the Culture and Language Academy of Success (CLAS) approach to a responsive learning environment.

This chapter examines eight research-based ingredients for a responsive learning environment developed and implemented at CLAS. This recipe shows what a responsive learning environment should look like. Many visitors to CLAS have been profoundly impressed by the learning environments CLAS staff members have created. These eight ingredients include:

1. A print-rich environment that is 70 percent authentic (student- or teacher-created) materials and 30 percent real-life materials

2. Learning centers for reading, writing, listening, math, science, and cultural exploration

3. Culturally colorful materials, such as ethnic cloths, prints, artwork, and artifacts

4. Optimally arranged spaces that allow for presentations and movement

5. Multiple libraries that include cultural, multicultural, content-specific, and reading-level-appropriate literature

6. Technology that is prominently displayed

7. Relevant bulletin boards that feature cultural materials, student work, current unit materials, current events, and content-area materials

8. Displayed student work and images of students that are current, ample, and unit related

These ingredients combine as they would in an actual recipe—without one element, the dish is incomplete. However, the exact amount of each ingredient and the mixture of the ingredients are left up to the cook's creativity, intuition, and experience. This intentional flexibility allows teachers to customize the learning environment to their unique students. In other words, the responsive environment should not be cookie-cutter or branded. Even though the components are prescriptive and defined, how the environment will ultimately look is descriptive, dependent, and highly reliant on the teacher to think outside of the box.

In this chapter, we offer a description of the ingredients and look at actual CLAS classrooms to provide a picture of what a responsive learning environment looks like.

A Print-Rich Environment

The importance of a print-rich environment has been well documented (Cunningham, 1995). Content-specific classrooms should be filled with print material that is representative of the subject area. Students should walk into the room and immediately know the focus of the class (for upper-level students) or the various subjects (for elementary students). We suggest a ratio of 70 percent authentic materials and 30 percent real-world materials. Authentic materials are those produced by students and teachers. Examples include samples of student work and writing and teacher materials such as word walls. Real-world materials are those print materials taken directly from real life, such as signs, maps, commercial literature (pages from newspapers and magazines), and so on. These materials engage students by helping them connect the word of school with their experiences outside of school in their homes and communities.

Learning Centers

Learning centers are a common recommendation in effective learning environments. It is important that teachers go beyond the traditional centers, however (such as reading, writing, and science). For example, listening centers and cultural centers provide a more unique experience for students. A litany of research has demonstrated how audio, namely music, helps to stimulate thinking and learning (Shade et al., 1997). Cultural music, such as Native American flute and American jazz, can assist in learning and also make connections to students' cultural heritage. At CLAS, we strongly encourage cultural centers, which are stocked with cultural items students bring in from their homes and communities. Students have the opportunity to write about these artifacts and of course "show and tell" frequently. The center acts as a living museum for the class and becomes a source of pride as each student, regardless of his or her culture, is expected to contribute. It is important to think in broad terms when designing these cultural centers. They can include items related to culture, gender, religion, and so on. Figure 11.1 (page 142) shows an example from CLAS of a listening center stocked with different musical instruments from various cultures that both students and the teacher provided.

Figure 11.1: A learning center with musical instruments from different cultures.

Another example comes from a school in Sacramento, California, where Sharroky observed a cast-iron black skillet in a classroom's cultural center. The student who made the contribution explained that it was his grandmother's and his parents told him stories about how she "used to cook everything in it." This anecdote demonstrates potential for validation and affirmation of students' cultural and familial backgrounds and at the same time encourages reflection on cultural history and storytelling, thus reinforcing literacy skills.

Culturally Colorful Materials

Often when we think of schools, the words *drab, dark, gray,* and *plain* come to mind. Those are not the colors at CLAS, where the rooms are bright, dynamic, lively, and inviting. Culturally colorful materials exude fun, friendliness, and excitement about learning. An inviting classroom uses color and lighting to engage students. It has been well documented in the business world that environment can actually facilitate employee productivity. This is the case for classrooms as well. For example, according to cognitive psychologist Barbara Shade and her colleagues, Native American cultures seem to prefer earth tones, and in some cases bright yellows and pastels (Shade et al., 1997). These colors, when brought to the classroom, connect students' home and community culture with school. At CLAS, some teachers have been known to request new colors in their classrooms or even offer to paint their own rooms during the summer months to make the environment livelier. If this isn't possible, then teachers can use wall borders, posters, signs, tapestries, murals, or other culturally relevant materials to create a positive mood, tempo, and vibe in the classroom. Figure 11.2 shows a reading center that also includes many culturally colorful materials, such as a tapestry, several posters, musical instruments, and sculptures from different cultures.

Figure 11.2: A reading center with culturally colorful materials.

Optimally Arranged Space

How to arrange the desks, tables, and chairs within a classroom is not an easy decision. Many teachers go through several room configurations during the course of the year before deciding on an optimal version. There is no one prescribed configuration, but responsive environments should promote movement and allow students to see the entire room. The arrangement of desks and tables should reflect the importance of interpersonal relationships in the classroom among students and between the student and the teacher. The traditional approach to classroom arrangement, "cemetery rows" of seats that all face the teacher, does not promote interpersonal relationships, including collaboration. In addition to spatial accommodation for collaborative groups, research suggests that it is just as important to have space where the students can connect individually with the teacher (Good & Brophy, 1977). Both of these components allow for a feeling of community, connectivity, and collaboration while providing students with space to work and learn.

Figure 11.3 shows a room at CLAS with optimally arranged space. Notice that tables and chairs are arranged in groups, rather than in traditional rows, with lots of space for students to work at their tables and move around the classroom. In this configuration, students are able to see all sides of the room, and there is ample space for work at the perimeter near posted learning stations.

Figure 11.3: A classroom configuration that allows for community, connectivity, and collaboration.

Multiple Libraries

A critical addition to any print-rich environment is many books organized into multiple libraries. These libraries can represent a variety of categories, such as genres, authors, topics, and reading levels. How the books are displayed is important as well. Similar to the notion of the culturally colorful classroom, libraries set up in a way that is inviting and enticing to students can make all the difference in supporting the students' interest in books and reading. The appeal of a display can be what brings a student into the library and engages him or her in the act of reading. A wide variety and large number of books are beneficial to students, especially underserved students who are not skilled readers, for three reasons: (1) they give students access to materials that they might not have in their homes and communities, (2) they give students wider choices for book selection, and (3) they give students multiple opportunities to practice their literacy skills, such as writing, speaking, and listening. When considering variety, we suggest you think beyond race and ethnic identity. Include these, but also books that explore gender, social, youth-oriented, and economic issues.

Technology

The pervasive use of technology is hard to miss in the typical classroom today. Many classrooms now come equipped with LCD projectors, document readers, and ActiveBoards, not to mention laptops for students and teachers. Technology can be responsive, especially if it is infused into the instruction frequently and with transparency. What we are promoting primarily here is the use of the available technology to enhance student learning. What we have found in our work with teachers, particularly in schools with high numbers of underserved students, is that while some schools are fully stocked with all the latest technology that is fully infused into the instruction, many other schools have stacks of technology with very little or no infusion. This latter scenario limits students' opportunities to be 21st century learners, which is particularly detrimental to students who might not have much access to technology outside of school in their homes and communities. Responsive pedagogy provides such opportunities.

At CLAS, technology is not only used, but it is kept in the open for students to see—not locked behind closed doors in computer rooms or classrooms students visit only infrequently. The idea is to make technology part of the everyday classroom and not something students use only when they attempt to find books in the library or write their papers.

Relevant Bulletin Boards

Teachers typically use bulletin boards for two reasons: to connect to the lesson or content being covered and to relate to the overall theme of the lesson. There is nothing wrong with this approach, but it is not always responsive—it does not necessarily speak to students in a responsive way through images that represent a variety of cultures, including youth culture. Infusing elements of youth culture and students' own home and community cultures into a bulletin board serves to draw students in to the topic. For example, at CLAS, a teacher might construct a bulletin board specifically about African proverbs and poetry during a broader poetry unit. Figure 11.4 shows what a board such as this might look like. It includes examples of poetry and proverbs from various countries using culturally colorful materials. Examples of bulletin boards that appeal to youth culture would be inspirational and motivational boards that include lyrics and photos from popular music artists or poets. Teachers should update and change their bulletin boards periodically to keep students engaged in the material.

Figure 11.4: A bulletin board that shows African poetry and proverbs.

Displayed Student Work and Images of Students

Promoting student work is part of responsive instruction. We all recall the warm feeling that goes with seeing our work displayed—the classroom's version of having your name in lights. We want all students to have that feeling because it is validating and affirming of their hard work. The recommendation at CLAS is that new student work should be displayed every three weeks. The work should be exemplary in nature but not exclusionary. Some students may not produce exemplary work for varying reasons, so it's important for teachers to display student work in a way that highlights everyone's work. When Sharroky was a classroom teacher, he made a point to be sure all students had their work displayed. He recalls many students—eighth graders—who had never had their work displayed in their classrooms. They were excited to see their work displayed, and students often became more engaged in projects that might be displayed because they felt the need to improve their skills and work.

In addition to student-produced materials, Geneva Gay (2000) notes that the most responsive images teachers can use in the classroom are images of the students themselves—specifically, images of students engaged in school activities. Students respond positively when they see themselves as part of the classroom. Images of students reading, writing, using technology, playing outside, and collaborating reinforce that all people in the school are part of a larger community of learners. Gay recommends the goal of having every child's image appear somewhere in the school at some point.

Building a Responsive Learning Environment

The learning environment survey (Hollie, 2011) in figure 11.5 (pages 148–149) is a useful tool teachers and schools can use to collect informal feedback to assess how responsive their learning environment is. Teachers can use the tool to assess their own individual classrooms, school leaders can use the tool during walk-thoughs, or grade-level teams can visit each other's classrooms and comment on the level of responsiveness they observe. The tool is intended to lead to discussion about the learning environment and how teachers could make improvements.

Learning Environment Survey

Print-Rich Environment

1. Is there a 70:30 ratio of authentic and commercially produced print-rich items? YES or NO (circle one)

2. Rate the level of responsiveness (creativity, presentation, and student friendliness).

Least Responsive				Very Responsive
1	2	3	4	5

Comments/Suggestions:

Learning Centers

3. Are a variety of learning centers present? YES or NO (circle one)

4. Rate the level of responsiveness (creativity, presentation, and student friendliness).

Least Responsive				Very Responsive
1	2	3	4	5

Comments/Suggestions:

Culturally Colorful Materials

5. Is the room filled with a variety of colorful materials that are culturally relevant and/or relevant to the school? YES or NO (circle one)

6. Rate the level of responsiveness (creativity, presentation, and student friendliness).

Least Responsive				Very Responsive
1	2	3	4	5

Comments/Suggestions:

Optimally Arranged Space

7. Is the room arranged optimally for movement, classroom management, and presentations? YES or NO (circle one)

8. Rate the level of responsiveness (creativity, presentation, and student friendliness).

Least Responsive				Very Responsive
1	2	3	4	5

Comments/Suggestions:

Multiple Libraries

9. Are there multiple libraries in the room that demonstrate a focus on multiple literacies? YES or NO (circle one)

10. Rate the level of responsiveness (creativity, presentation, and student friendliness).

    Least Responsive   Very Responsive
    1   2   3   4   5

    Comments/Suggestions:

Technology

11. Is technology present and ready for use? YES or NO (circle one)

12. Rate the level of responsiveness (creativity, presentation, and student friendliness).

    Least Responsive   Very Responsive
    1   2   3   4   5

    Comments/Suggestions:

Bulletin Boards

13. Are the bulletin boards relevant to content areas and student culture? YES or NO (circle one)

14. Rate the level of responsiveness (creativity, presentation, and student friendliness).

    Least Responsive   Very Responsive
    1   2   3   4   5

    Comments/Suggestions:

Student Work and Images

15. Is student work displayed throughout the room—both exemplary and nonexemplary work? YES or NO (circle one)

16. Does the room contain images of students? YES or NO (circle one)

17. Rate the level of responsiveness (creativity, presentation, and student friendliness).

    Least Responsive   Very Responsive
    1   2   3   4   5

    Comments/Suggestions:

Figure 11.5: Learning environment survey.

Learning environments are students' first experience of school when they walk into the room at the beginning of the school year. We believe eight ingredients come together to create a "recipe for success." We must remember that there is always room for teacher creativity in creating the learning environment. This behavior becomes instinctive once the right professional culture is connected to the right professional skill. Reflect on the questions that follow as you consider your learning environment.

CHAPTER 11

Reflections

1   How do you currently use your environment to enhance instruction?

2   To what extent are there resources available to improve your learning environment?

3   Based on the survey of your learning environment, which of your areas is most in need?

4   Based on the survey of your learning environment, which area is least in need?

Afterword

As researchers, consultants, and educators, we have dedicated our lives to helping schools improve. Obviously, we have a professional interest in seeing our work lead to school improvement, but we also have a personal interest. As African American men who grew up in Flint, Michigan (Anthony), and Los Angeles, California (Sharroky), we both have witnessed capable friends perish in the status quo of the American school system. This is unacceptable to us. We want to challenge the traditional system to reflect on its views and perceptions about underserved students. Are students the problem, or are our perceptions about and structures for teaching students the problem?

All human beings want to be successful. This desire has to be cultivated in an environment that embraces, validates, and supports students, not one in which they are discriminated against. We want school staffs to challenge and condemn the racism, the classism, the sexism, and all forms of discrimination that interferes with their expectations for student performance. Every student deserves a healthy learning environment.

We want educators to reflect on their pedagogy. Do the activities they use serve students' needs? Do they affirm the students' culture? Do they build on a set of skills that the students bring to school with them? Students deserve teachers who have a responsive pedagogy that best meets their needs and develops them intellectually. All students can learn, but they must be taught in the manner that they learn best.

Finally, we challenge teachers and school leaders to break the norm of underachievement for poor and minority students. Educators are in the best position to change this reality. Equality appears to be a quality that most people embrace conceptually but not in reality. Schools can be the great equalizer if the educators within them have the will to lead and the skill to teach.

References and Resources

73% say being a teacher is one of the most important jobs. (2010). *Rasmussen Reports.* Accessed at www.rasmussenreports.com/public_content/lifestyle/general_lifestyle /may_2010/73_say_being_a_teacher_is_one_of_the_most_important_jobs on December 4, 2010.

Akey, T. M. (2006). *School context, student attitudes and behavior, and academic achievement: An exploratory analysis.* New York: MDRC.

Alicke, M. D., Braun, J. C., Glor, J. E., Klotz, M. L., Magee, J., Sederhoim, H., & Siegel, R. (1992). Complaining behavior in social interaction. *Personality and Social Psychology Bulletin, 18*(3), 286–295.

Allen, J. (1999). *Words, words, words: Teaching vocabulary 4–12.* Portland, ME: Stenhouse.

Alloway, K., & Runquist, J. M. (2010, January 14). More than 800 N. J. schools failed to meet No Child Left Behind standards. *The Star-Ledger,* p. 1.

Annie E. Casey Foundation. (2011). *2011 kids count data book.* Baltimore, MD: Author.

Associated Press. (2003, January 29). *Report: Teacher retention biggest school woe.* Accessed at www.cnn.com/2003/education/01/029/teacher.shortage.ap on February 30, 2003.

August, D., & Shanahan, T. (Eds.). (2006). *Developing literacy in second-language learners: A report of the National Literacy Panel on Language-Minority Children and Youth.* Mahwah, NJ: Lawrence Erlbaum.

Bakst, B. (2008, March 19). States to get leeway on school sanctions. *USA Today.* Accessed at www.usatoday.com/news/nation/2008–03–19–2917642418_x.htm on August 17, 2011.

Baldoni, J. (2007). Leadership: trust matters [Web log entry]. *Fast Company.* Accessed at www .fastcompany.com/blog/john-baldoni/grab-n-go-leadership/leadership-trust-matters on May 2, 2011.

Barnes, G., Crowe, E., & Schaefer, B. (n.d.). *The cost of teacher turnover in five school districts: A pilot study.* Washington, DC: National Commission on Teaching and America's Future.

Beck, I. L., McKeown, M. G., & Kucan, L. (2002). *Bringing words to life.* New York: Guilford Press.

Becker, G. S. (1983). A theory of competition among pressure groups for political influence. *Quarterly Journal of Economics, 98*(13), 371–400.

Bennett, B. (2010). The artful science of instructional integration. In R. Marzano (Ed.), *On excellence in teaching* (pp. 65–91). Bloomington, IN: Solution Tree Press.

Blume, H. (2010, February 12). L.A. unified schools chief works for district supplier. *Los Angeles Times.* p. 1.

Bolman, L. G., & Deal, T. E. (1995). *Leading with soul: An uncommon journey of spirit.* San Francisco: Jossey-Bass.

Bowles, S., & Gintis, H. (1976). *Schooling in capitalist America: Educational reform and the contradictions of economic life.* New York: Basic Books.

Braeden, M. C. (2008, February 6). Teacher quality gap examined worldwide. *Education Week.*

Brown, E. R. (2009). *Educator perceptions of NCLB legislation and its impact on character education.* Unpublished doctoral dissertation, Immaculata College.

Brunsma, D. L. (2004). *The school uniform movement and what it tells us about American education: A symbolic crusade.* Lanham, MD: ScarecrowEducation.

Buffum, A., Erkens, C., Hinman, C., Huff, S., Jessie, L. G., Martin, T., et al. (2008). *The collaborative administrator: Working together as a professional learning community.* Bloomington, IN: Solution Tree Press.

Butler, J. A., & Dickson, K. M. (1987). *Snapshot #2: Improving school culture—Centennial High School* (School Improvement Research Series, Snapshot #2). Accessed at http://educationnorthwest.org/webfm_send/517 on August 17, 2011.

Carleton, L., & Marzano, R. (2010). *Vocabulary games for the classroom.* Bloomington, IN: Marzano Research Laboratory.

Carpenter, C. (2011, March 31). WNC Teachers to Shuler: NCLB should be fixed or nixed. *Macon County News.* Accessed at www.maconnews.com/news/education/629-wnc-teachers-to-shuler-nclb-must-be-fixed-or-nixed on August 17, 2011.

Carpenter, J., & Hilliard, S. (2005). Shifting parameters of individual and group variation: African American English on Roanoke Island. *Journal of English Linguistics, 33*(2), 161–184.

Carpenter, W. A. (2000). Ten years of silver bullets: Dissenting thoughts on education reform. *Phi Delta Kappan, 81*(5), 383–389.

Christensen, C. M., Horn, M. B., & Johnson, C. W. (2008). *Disrupting class: How disruptive innovation will change the way the world learns.* New York: McGraw-Hill.

Collins, J. (2001). *Good to great: Why some companies make the leap . . . and others don't.* New York: HarperBusiness.

Connell, R. W. (1993). *Schools and social justice.* Philadelphia: Temple University Press.

Cort, R., Field, T., Nolin, M. (Producers), & Herek, S. (Director). (1995). *Mr. Holland's opus* [Motion picture]. United States: Hollywood Pictures.

Covey, S. R. (1989). *The seven habits of highly effective people: Restoring the character ethic.* New York: Simon & Schuster.

Cromwell, S. (2002). Is your school culture toxic or positive? *Education World, 6*(2).

Cummings, C. (1996). *Teaching makes a difference* (2nd ed.). Edmonds, WA: Teaching, Inc.

Cunningham, P. (1995). *Phonics they use: Words for reading and writing* (2nd ed.). New York: HarperCollins.

Danielson, C. (2007). *Enhancing professional practice: A framework for teaching* (2nd ed.). Alexandria, VA: Association for Supervision and Curriculum Development.

Deal, T. E., & Peterson, K. D. (1999). *Shaping school culture: The heart of leadership.* San Francisco: Jossey-Bass.

De Pree, M. (1989). *Leadership is an art.* New York: Doubleday.

Dewan, S. (2010). Experts say schools need to screen for cheating. *New York Times.* Accessed at www.nytimes.com/2010/02/13/education/13erase.html on May 2, 2011.

Doublet, S. (2000). *The stress myth.* Chesterfield, MO: Science & Humanities Press.

DuFour, R. (2001). Community: Getting everyone to buy in. *Journal of Staff Development, 22*(4). Accessed at www.learningforward.org/news/jsd/dufour224.cfm on August 17, 2011.

DuFour, R., & DuFour, R. (2006). The power of professional learning communities. *National Forum of Educational Administration and Supervision Journal, 24*(1), 2–5.

DuFour, R., DuFour, R., & Eaker, R. (2008). *Revisiting professional learning communities at work: New insights for improving schools.* Bloomington, IN: Solution Tree Press.

DuFour, R., DuFour, R., Eaker, R., & Karhanek, G. (2010). *Raising the bar and closing the gap: Whatever it takes.* Bloomington, IN: Solution Tree Press.

DuFour, R., & Eaker, R. (1998). *Professional learning communities at work: Best practices for enhancing student achievement.* Bloomington, IN: National Education Service.

Earl, L., & Katz, S. (2006). *Leading schools in a data rich world: Harnessing data for school improvement.* Thousand Oaks, CA: Corwin Press.

Echevarria, J., & Graves, A. (2011). *Sheltered content instruction: Teaching students with diverse needs* (4th ed.). Boston: Pearson.

Emmer, E. T., Sanford, J. P., Clements, B. S., & Martin, J. (1982). *Improving classroom management and organization in junior high schools: An experimental investigation* (Research and Development Center for Teacher Education Rep. No. 6153). Austin: Research and Development Center for Teacher Education, University of Texas.

Emmer, E. T., Evertson, C. M., & Worsham, M. E. (2003). *Classroom management for secondary teachers* (6th ed.). Boston: Allyn & Bacon.

Evans, R. (1996). *The human side of change: Reform, resistance, and the real-life problems of innovation.* San Francisco: Jossey-Bass.

Feller, B. (2006, April 20). *AP poll: Teachers dubious of "no child."* Accessed at www.highbeam.com/doc/1P1-122146681.html on August 17, 2011.

Ferguson, R. F. (1998). Teachers' perceptions and expectations and the *Black-White* test score gap. *Urban Education, 38*(4), 460–507.

Ferrera, R. J. (2005). Accountability alarms: Educators need to pay attention to some alarms that might be sounding in their schools and districts as they seek accountability through assessment. *Leadership, 35*(2), 24.

Franken, A. (2010). Principal quality essential for student success. *Hometown Source.* Accessed at https://hometownsource.com/2010/01/26/principal-quality-essential-for-student-success-says-sen-franken/ on May 2, 2011.

Frayer, D., Frederick, W. C., & Klausmeier, H. J. (1969). *A schema for testing the level of cognitive mastery.* Madison: Wisconsin Center for Education Research.

Fullan, M. (2003). *The moral imperative of school leadership.* Thousand Oaks, CA: Corwin Press.

Fullan, M. (2008). *The six secrets of change: What the best leaders do to help their organizations survive and thrive.* San Francisco: Jossey-Bass.

Fyans, L. J., & Maehr, M. L. (1990). *"School culture," student ethnicity, and motivation.* Urbana, IL: The National Center for School Leadership.

Gardner, J. W. (1998). *Leadership: An overview.* Washington, DC: Leadership Studies Program, Independent Sector.

Gay, G. (2000). *Culturally responsive teaching: Theory, research, and practice.* New York: Teachers College Press.

Glasser, W. (1998). *Choice theory: A new psychology of personal freedom.* New York: HarperCollins.

Goddard, R. D., Hoy, W. K. , & Hoy, A. W. (2000). Collective teacher efficacy: Its meaning, measure, and effect on student achievement. *American Education Research Journal, 37*(2), 479–507.

Goffman, E. (1959). *The presentation of self in everyday life.* Garden City, NY: Doubleday.

Good, T. L., & Brophy, J. E. (1977). *Educational psychology: A realistic approach.* New York: Holt, Rinehart and Winston.

Gordon, R., Piana, L. D., & Keleher, T. (2000). *Facing the consequences: An examination of racial discrimination in the U.S. public schools.* Oakland, CA: ERASE Initiative, Applied Research Center.

Graves, M. F. (2006). *The vocabulary book: Learning & instruction.* New York: Teachers College Press.

Green, R. L. (2005). *Expectations: How teacher expectations can increase student achievement and assist in closing the achievement gap.* Columbus, OH: SRA/McGraw-Hill.

Harris, V. J. (Ed.). (1999). *Teaching multicultural literature in grades K–8.* Norwood, MA: Christopher-Gordon.

Hattie, J. A. C. (2009). *Visible learning: A synthesis of over 800 meta-analyses relating to achievement.* New York: Routledge.

Herrnstein, R. J., & Murray, C. (1994). *The bell curve: Intelligence and class structure in American life.* New York: Free Press.

Hollie, S. (2011). *Culturally and linguistically responsive teaching and learning: Classroom practices for student success.* Huntington Beach, CA: Shell Education.

hooks, b. (2003). *Rock my soul: Black people and self-esteem.* New York: Atria Books.

Howard, G. R. (2006). *We can't teach what we don't know: White teachers, multiracial schools.* New York: Teachers College Press.

"Illiteracy: The Downfall of American Society." (2011, June 13). Accessed at http://education -portal.com/articles/Illiteracy_The_Downfall_of_American_Society.html on September 5, 2011.

Institute for Educational Leadership. (2000). *Leadership for student learning: Reinventing the principalship.* Washington, DC: Author.

Jacobson, L. (2008). NCLB restructuring found ineffectual in California. *Education Week, 27*(24), 15, 17.

Jensen, E. (2003). *Teaching with the brain in mind.* Alexandria, VA: Association for Supervision and Curriculum Development.

Jensen, E. (2005). *Teaching with the brain in mind* (2nd ed.). Alexandria, VA: Association for Supervision and Curriculum Development.

Kagan, S., & Kagan, M. (2009). *Kagan cooperative learning.* San Clemente, CA: Kagan Publishing.

Katzenmeyer, M., & Moller, G. (2001). *Awakening the sleeping giant: Helping teachers develop as leaders* (2nd ed.). Thousand Oaks, CA: Corwin Press.

Kennedy, M. (2005). *Inside teaching: How classroom life undermines reform.* Cambridge, MA: Harvard University Press.

Kohn. A. (1996). *Beyond discipline: From compliance to community.* Alexandria, VA: Association for Supervision and Curriculum Development.

Kopkowski, C. (2008). Why they leave. *NEA Today.* Accessed at www.nea.org/home/12630 .htm on May 2, 2011.

Kotulak, R. (1996). *Inside the brain: Revolutionary discoveries of how the mind works.* Kansas City, MO: Andrews and McMeel.

Kramer, U. (2010). Coping and defense mechanisms: What's the difference?—Second act. *Psychology and Psychotherapy, 87*(2), 207–221.

Krashen, S. D. (2004). *The power of reading: Insights from the research.* Westport, CT: Libraries Unlimited.

Langlois, J. H., Kalakanis, L., Rubenstein, A. J., Larson, A., Hallam, M., & Smoot, M. (2000). Maxims or myths of beauty? A meta-analytic and theoretical review. *Psychological Bulletin, 126*(3), 390–423.

LeMoine, N. (1998). *English for your success.* Maywood, NJ: People's Publishing.

Lemov, D. (2010). *Teach like a champion: 49 techniques that put students on the path to college.* San Francisco: Jossey-Bass.

Lezotte, L. W. (2010). Revolutionary and evolutionary: The effective schools movement. *Edutopia.* Accessed at www.edutopia.org/pdfs/edutopia.org-closing-achievement -gap-lezotte-article.pdf on May 2, 2011.

Marzano, R. J. (2009a). *Designing and teaching learning goals and objectives: Classroom strategies that work.* Bloomington, IN: Marzano Research Laboratory.

Marzano, R. J. (2009b). *Getting serious about school reform: Three critical commitments.* Bloomington, IN: Marzano Research Laboratory.

Marzano, R. J. (Ed.). (2010). *On excellence in teaching.* Bloomington, IN: Solution Tree Press.

Marzano, R. J., Marzano, J. S., & Pickering, D. J. (2003). *Classroom management that works: Research-based strategies for every teacher.* Alexandria, VA: Association for Supervision and Curriculum Development.

Marzano, R. J., & Waters, T. (2009). *District leadership that works: Striking the right balance.* Bloomington, IN: Solution Tree Press.

Maslow, A. H. (1943). A theory of human motivation. *Psychological Review, 50*(4), 370–396.

McLaughlin, M., & Talbert, J. (2006). *Building school-based teacher learning communities: Professional strategies to improve student achievement.* New York: Teachers College, Columbia University.

Moir, E. (2008). Building an effective new teacher support system. *NEA Today,* June 2009, p. 4.

Moos, R. H. (1979). *Evaluating educational environments.* San Francisco: Jossey-Bass.

Muhammad, A. (2006). Do we believe that they can learn? *National Forum of Educational Administration and Supervision Journal, 24*(1), 14–20.

Muhammad, A. (2006/2007). Educators must accept the challenge to be professional. *Leading Change, 5*(2), 14.

Muhammad, A. (2008). Teaching matters: Leadership that improves professional practice. In A. Buffum, C. Erkens, C. Hinman, S. Huff, L. G. Jessie, T. Martin, et al. (Eds.), *The collaborative administrator: Working together as a professional learning community* (pp. 127–142). Bloomington, IN: Solution Tree Press.

Muhammad, A. (2009). *Transforming school culture: How to overcome staff division.* Bloomington, IN: Solution Tree Press.

National Association for the Advancement of Colored People. (2011). *Misplaced priorities: Over incarcerate, under educate.* Washington, DC: Author.

New America Foundation. (2008). *Changing the odds for children at risk.* Accessed at www .newamerica.net/events/2008/changing_odds on May 3, 2011.

Norton, T., & Land, B. (2007). *50 Literacy strategies for beginning teachers, 1–8* (2nd ed.). Upper Saddle River, NJ: Prentice Hall.

Ogbu, J. U. (1978). *Minority educations and caste: The American system in cross cultural perspective.* New York: Academic Press.

Ogbu, J. U. (2003). *Black American students in an affluent suburb: A study of academic disengagement.* Mahwah, NJ: Lawrence Erlbaum Associates.

Orr, J. (2009). Our top ten favorite John Wooden quotes. *Christian Science Monitor.* Accessed at www.csmonitor.com/USA/Politics/The-Vote/2009/1014/our-top-ten-favorite-john -wooden-quotes on May 2, 2011.

Palincsar, A. S. (1986). Reciprocal teaching. In *Teaching reading as thinking.* Oak Brook, IL: North Central Regional Educational Laboratory.

Patterson, K., Grenny, J., McMillan, R., & Switzler, A. (2002). *Crucial conversations: Tools for talking when stakes are high.* New York: McGraw-Hill.

Penuel, W., Fishman, B., Yamaguchi, R., & Gallagher, L. (2007). What makes professional development effective? Strategies that foster curriculum implementation. *American Education Research Journal, 44*(4), 921–958.

Petrides, L., & Nodine, T. (2005). *Anatomy of school system improvement: Performance-driven practices in urban school districts.* San Francisco: New Schools Venture Fund.

Piestrup, A. M. (1973). *Black dialect interference and accommodation of reading instruction in first grade.* Berkeley: University of California.

Porter, L. W. (1961). A study of perceived need satisfaction in bottom and middle management jobs. *Journal of Applied Psychology, 45*(1), 1–10.

Ravitch, D. (2010, November 10). The myth of charter schools. *The New York Review of Books.* Accessed at www.nybooks.com/articles/archives/2010/nov/11/myth-charter-schools/ on September 12, 2011.

Reeves, D. B. (2000). *Accountability in action: A blueprint for learning organizations.* Denver, CO: Advanced Learning Press.

Shade, B., Kelly, C., & Oberg, M. (1997). *Creating culturally responsive classrooms.* Washington, DC: American Psychological Association.

Shaw, B. (2008). Our nation still at risk. *Education Week, 27*(27), 26.

Sheppard, B., Brown, J., & Dibbon, D. (2008). *School district leadership matters.* New York: Springer.

Sparks, D. (2002). High-performing cultures increase teacher retention. *Results.* Accessed at www.learningforward.org/news/results/res12-02spar.cfm on May 2, 2011.

Sparks, S. (2010). Study finds bad schools rarely get better—or shut down. *Education Week, 30*(15), 3.

Stahl, S. A. (1999). *Vocabulary development.* Cambridge, MA: Brookline Books.

Stolp, S. (1994). *Leadership for school culture.* Accessed at www.eric.ed.gov/PDFS /ED370198.pdf on May 5, 2011. (ERIC Document Reproduction Service No. ED370198)

Taylor, F. W. (1947). *Scientific management: Comprising shop management, the principles of scientific management [and] testimony before the special House committee.* New York: Harper.

Thacker, J. L., & McInerney, W. (1992). Changing academic culture to improve student achievement in the elementary schools. *ERS Spectrum, 10*(4), 18–23.

Thornburgh, N. (2006). Dropout nation. *Time.* Accessed at www.time.com/time/magazine /article/0,9171,1181646,00.html on May 3, 2011.

Toppo, G. (2003). The face of the American teacher: White and female while her students are ethnically diverse. *USA Today.* Accessed at www.usatoday.com/educate/college/education /articles/20030706.htm on May 3, 2011.

Trelease, J. (2001). *The read-aloud handbook* (5th ed.). New York: Penguin Books.

Tyack, D., & Cuban, L. (1995). *Tinkering toward utopia: A century of public school reform.* Cambridge, MA: Harvard University Press.

U. S. Department of Education. (2005a). *10 facts about K–12 education funding.* Washington, DC: Author.

U.S. Department of Education. (2005b). *Eight questions on teacher recruitment and retention: What does the research say?* Washington, DC: Author.

Vandenberghe, R., & Huberman, A. M. (Eds.). (1999). *Understanding and preventing teacher burnout: A sourcebook of international research and practice.* Cambridge, UK: Cambridge University Press.

Viadero, D. (2008). Teachers advised to "get real" on race. *Education Week, 27*(21), 1.

Viadero, D. (2010). Study finds wide achievement gaps for top students. *Education Week, 29*(21), 6.

Webb, C. (1993). Teacher perceptions of professional development needs and the implementation of the K–6 science and technology syllabus. *Research in Science Education, 23*(1), 327–336.

Wilson, B. L., & Corbett, H. D. (2001). *Listening to urban kids: School reform and the teachers they want.* Albany: State University of New York Press.

Wolfe, P. (2001). *Brain matters: Translating research into classroom practice.* Alexandria, VA: Association for Supervision and Curriculum Development.

Wren, D. J. (1999). School culture: Exploring the hidden curriculum. *Adolescence, 34*(135), 593–596.

Index

Transforming School Culture: How to Overcome Staff Division
Anthony Muhammad
Busy administrators will appreciate this quick read packed with immediate, accessible strategies for transforming toxic school cultures into healthy environments conducive to change. **BKF281**

Transforming School Culture: Understanding and Overcoming Resistance to Necessary Change
Featuring Anthony Muhammad
Discover the underlying tensions that impact school culture by exploring four different types of educators: Believers, Fundamentalists, Tweeners, and Survivors. **DVF022**

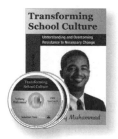

The Power of Professional Learning Communities at Work™: Bringing the Big Ideas to Life
Featuring Richard DuFour, Robert Eaker, and Rebecca DuFour
This video series explores eight diverse schools, where teachers and administrators engage in candid conversations and collaborative meetings. See how successful schools radically improve student learning as you learn the fundamentals of PLC. **DVF052**

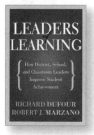

Leaders of Learning: How District, School, and Classroom Leaders Improve Student Achievement
Richard DuFour and Robert J. Marzano
The authors examine how district leadership, principal leadership, team leadership, and effective teachers can improve student achievement. **BKF455**

Solution Tree | Press

a division of

Solution Tree

Visit solution-tree.com or call 800.733.6786 to order.

Wait! Your professional development journey doesn't have to end with the last pages of this book.

We realize improving student learning doesn't happen overnight. And your school or district shouldn't be left to puzzle out all the details of this process alone.

No matter where you are on the journey, we're committed to helping you get to the next stage.

Take advantage of everything from **custom workshops** to **keynote presentations** and **interactive web and video conferencing**. We can even help you develop an action plan tailored to fit your specific needs.

Let's get the conversation started.

Call 888.763.9045 today.